MAKE THE MOST OF
TOWN & CITY GARDENING

MAKE THE MOST OF
TOWN & CITY GARDENING

TREASURE PRESS

First published in 1983 under the title
Not Just Small But Tiny by
Phoebe Phillips / Heinemann

This edition published in 1985 by
Chancellor Press
59 Grosvenor Street
London W1

Edited and designed by
Phoebe Phillips Editions

ISBN 0 907486 77 0

Printed in Hong Kong

To my long-suffering wife Barbara and daughters Tamsin and Sophie

CONTENTS

INTRODUCTION

Town and City Gardening is intended for any-one, in town or country, who gardens in a limited space. The largest designs are small – back gardens only 15ft x 15ft (about 4½m x 4½m). The smallest are truly tiny – hanging baskets, some less than a foot square (about 0.09 square metres). Between these two extremes there are balconies and front doors, basements and roof gardens, front gardens, window boxes and side passage-ways.

In designing these gardens I have been concerned first with plants – their rela-tionship with each other and with hard sur-faces like walls, fences, paths and paving. Suggestions feature plants that will thrive in given situations: sun, shade or a mixture of both, high wind areas like roof gardens, and under the drip of trees. All should be avail-able from nurseries and plant stores. Alternative types and varieties can be found readily, so the plans can be adapted.

To help you find suitable and attractive plants I have positioned them in different types of gardens in and around different kinds of houses. The overall designs are not elaborate, but some architectural details are included to give a sense of style and period to the plans, and stimulate you to transform your own tiny garden with professional guidance.

Rather than specifying aspects – north, south, east or west – which don't always apply in very small gardens, I have indi-cated, where relevant, whether a garden is sunny, shaded or a mixture of both.

The first part of the book concentrates on basics: equipment and storage, building materials and structures, the right soil, con-tainers, propagation and feeding.

The second, major, part consists of more than 200 designs arranged by order around the house. Each chapter starts with a section on Style and Structure pointing out the potential – and potential problems – in each area, and giving practical advice on possible design elements and types of plants. This is followed by a section called Green Skeleton, evergreen plants and others that keep their shape even in winter, and provide a framework for your garden throughout the year – always important in a limited area. Spaces for seasonal plantings are indicated in each plan.

Except for two, Basements and Side Passageways, which have particular problems, designs are divided into seasons, and a number of plans are followed through from spring to winter so that you can see just how they will look throughout the year. The introductions to the seasonal sections have additional information about tasks to be car-ried out during the period. Each chapter also includes a number of individual designs for people with particular interests: edible or scented gardens, plans based on a single type of plant, designs with children, pets or easy maintenance in mind. Some relate to a

```
ABBREVIATIONS

in. = inches
ft  = feet
cm  = centimetre
m   = metre
oz  = ounces
lb  = pounds
kg  = kilograms
```

particular season, others – Specials – are more general. All the illustrations show how good-quality plants will have established themselves after two or three seasons.

Meticulous management and aftercare are essential to establish new plants, and I have included advice on these subjects in the descriptions of the illustrations, as well as in the seasonal introductions. However, gardening is very much a matter of common sense, and many aspects will become obvious once you know what you are trying to achieve. For example, a plant that must be trimmed to a compact shape in a window box may be allowed to spread in a larger space. The need for adequate watering cannot be over emphasized (particularly when plants are in containers or artificially small beds).

Always assess all aspects of your garden before you start to plan it. The main points to check with tiny areas are obvious. Are hanging baskets in dense shade – or bright sunlight? What colours and textures predominate in the background walls? If you are planning a window box, you may want to reflect an architectural detail in the box itself, and the style of the house – classic or cottagey – in the shape of the planting. Larger areas like back and front gardens are more complicated. You will have to check the number of mature plants that are already established, and how – or if – they can be incorporated in your design.

Decide on an overall budget, whatever the size of your garden – and be sure to allocate as large a proportion as possible to plants. They are by far the most important element in the majority of gardens – yet a surprising number of people will spend most of their budget on containers, equipment and garden furniture.

Although Latin names have their own fascination – and enable gardeners throughout the world to speak a common language – they can be puzzling to novices. Where possible I have given common names, followed by the full botanical description in italics – that is, the *genus* (which can include a large number of different plants that are botanically similar); the *species* (the actual plant within the *genus*); and sometimes the variety or type. If the third name is in quotation marks, and not in italic, the plant is a cultivar and first arose in cultivation. If there is no *species* name, and the *genus* is followed by a name in quotation marks this generally means that the plant is a hybrid, or a variety well known to nurserymen.

Common names are repeated without the botanical names after the first mention in any chapter, and both are cross-indexed at the back of the book for easy reference. If there is no common name, I give only the *genus* when the plant is repeated as above. Occasionally, I have given only *genus* names when your choice will best be guided by local stores and nurseries.

Finally, although the designs are divided into specific sections, many can be combined or used in others. Hanging baskets decorate porches and roof gardens as well as outside walls; window boxes can brighten side passageways and balconies as well as house fronts; container plantings can be used in a variety of areas. Treat the book as a giant jigsaw puzzle, using 'pieces' from different chapters, to create your own very small garden.

Michael Miller

EQUIPMENT

Although tiny gardens require less equipment than larger ones, this does not mean that you should sacrifice quality as well as quantity. Always buy the best you can afford, from reputable manufacturers.

Tools

A basic trowel and hand fork are essential. Stainless steel ones are easy to keep clean and slide through the soil. Here it's particularly important to spend as much money as you can afford – very cheap products simply bend when you use them to break up compacted soil. And choose handles with rounded tops to avoid too many blisters.

A narrow trowel is useful for weeding and planting bulbs, while a small shovel for spooning peat into containers will save time. Small border forks and spades are ideally suited to tiny gardens.

Keep an oily rag in your storage space and wipe tools with it when you have finished with them. This prevents rusting, and also makes tools easier to use the next time.

You will need a sprayer for applying insecticides, fungicides, foliar feeds and weed-killers. Buy the smallest of the pressurized units; hand-automated sprayers are only suitable for the smallest jobs. Whichever model you buy, always wash it very thoroughly after use, especially if you have been applying weed-killer.

A pair of pruning shears is necessary for tidying tree and shrub shapes, pruning, and removing spent flowers. Two types are available: the anvil, with the blade closing onto a static face; and the scissor-action type where the blades cross. In addition, a small pruning saw may be necessary for thick stems and branches.

Staking and tying back

Proper materials are essential; they enable you to stake plants professionally, and are inexpensive compared with the plants themselves. Canes and wooden stakes come in various lengths; remember that it's best to overestimate rather than underestimate the height plants will reach. A variety of ties and tying materials are on the market. The traditional soft green string is generally suitable for all but the heaviest of tying jobs, when plastic-coated wire or a proprietary tree-tie should be used.

'Vine eyes' can be used to fix wire to walls, while lead-headed wall nails encourage self-clinging plants onto the surfaces, but both are only suitable for softer brickwork. Use masonry nails for hard or rendered surfaces. Plain galvanized wire, available in several thicknesses, is the best type for wall climbers or shrubs. It will be less obtrusive if it follows the lines of the horizontal and vertical brick joints.

Plastic mesh is less aesthetically pleasing, but perfect for scrambling plants like clematis. It can be easily fixed to the wall with nails and wire or patented clips, but be sure to line it up with an architectural feature such as the top of a doorway.

Pest control

An enormous number of insecticides and fungicides are available. Take the advice of your local nursery or garden store, but be sure to follow the manufacturer's instructions – and keep the product in a safe place. Slugs can be killed with pellets or liquid.

Watering

Watering is the secret of success for small gardens and container plants. Make the task as easy as possible, with an exterior tap and a bracket on which to hang the hose. The new compact hose systems take up much less space than conventional types, but make sure the hose will reach within 4 feet (just over a metre) of the end of your garden, and from a tap to the balcony.

Many gardeners find that partially covering the open end of a hose pipe with the thumb produces as many spray patterns as they need – and has the advantage that the full flow is immediately available to soak plants and borders when necessary. Most watering problems are the result of keeping the nozzle in a fine-spray position and not allowing enough time for the water to penetrate the soil.

All kinds of conventional watering cans are available in garden stores, but it is worth while investing in one of the models used by professional gardeners. They are beautifully balanced, and make all the difference if you have boxes or pots that are difficult to reach.

Additional equipment

Put light garden rubbish in conventional plastic bags for easy disposal. If you have to get rid of tougher twigs and branches try to obtain larger, heavy-duty sacks that won't tear easily.

A waist-height apron with a capacious pocket protects clothes, and holds twine, etc. Gloves are essential for pruning, but your fingers will lack that certain 'feel' if you wear them for delicate potting or planting. Many gardeners use ordinary household rubber gloves for these jobs.

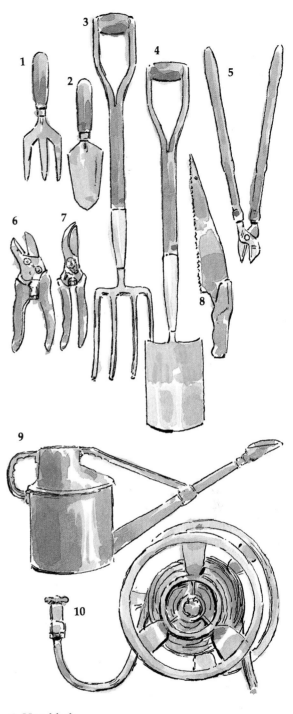

1. Hand fork.
2. Trowel.
3. Border fork.
4. Border spade.
5. Heavy-duty pruning shears.
6. Anvil-type pruning shears.
7. Scissor-action pruning shears.
8. Pruning saw.
9. Watering can.
10. Hose pipe and reel.

STORAGE

The illustrations on these pages show how storage space for tools and equipment can be both attractive and practical in a tiny space.

The following general points apply to all types of storage.

- Always buy exterior quality sheet material. Standard 'blockboard' deteriorates rapidly outdoors.

- It is preferable to stain timber (in one of the many colours available) rather than paint it. The only exception is when you want to match the colour with other painted areas.

- Storage units must be as waterproof as possible. Make sure that flat surfaces have drip edges, and put drip mouldings on vertical surfaces and on the bases of doors.

- However efficient your waterproofing, most units will be damp, if not wet, during winter. Clothing, fertilizers and other powdered materials will deteriorate if left outdoors.

Other suggestions for storage include a cupboard built under steps, with racks for tools, gardening shoes and other equipment, and a container, rather like a chest without its back, built across the 'dead-end' of a side passage. If all else fails it's well worth while building a cupboard in the kitchen, next to the back door, or converting an existing one for gardening tools and materials.

Plywood seat/storage space: 1. Hardwood edging acts as a drip channel. **2.** Overhang. **3.** Hardwood bead hides the edge of the plywood. Bearers (unseen) raise the base above the ground.

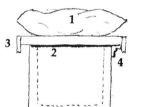

Detail: 1. Cushion. **2.** Optional rubber seal between base and lid. **3.** Hardwood edging. **4.** Hinge allows the lid to be lifted to a 90° angle.

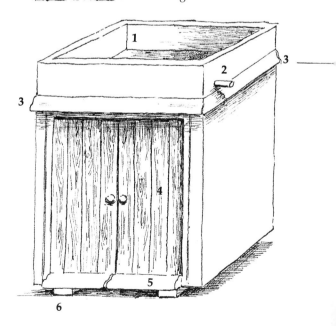

Brick rubbish enclosure: 1. The recessed top forms a planter. **2.** Drainage holes for planter. **3.** Wall, at a 45° angle, allows for easy access. **4.** Paving stones must drain away from the enclosure so that it can be hosed out.

Left: Timber cupboard. **1.** Planter top with metal liner. **2.** Copper overflow pipe from liner's base. **3.** A standard 'drip' moulding also acts as a design feature. **4.** Recessed doors. **5.** Drip moulding. **6.** Bearers raise the cupboard above the ground.

Right: Rubbish enclosure, as above, with simple wooden door instead of angled wall.

MATERIALS AND CONTAINERS

Different kinds of plants require different soils. Their preferences are usually given in catalogues, and soil-testing kits, which indicate the degree of alkalinity or acidity of the soil (the PH), are available from most nurseries. Soils are normally classified as chalk (highly alkaline), gravel, clay, loam, sand, peat (acid), or a mixture of these. It is possible to modify soil conditions: adding peat or leaf mould to an alkaline soil will reduce alkalinity, while adding lime to an acid soil reduces acidity.

One of the major advantages of a tiny garden is that there is less soil to be modified; and that containers, which can be filled with soil mixtures of your choice, fit naturally into small spaces.

The growing medium must give maximum benefit to plants, providing nutrients to the roots and some anchorage for the entire plant. Plant roots also absorb oxygen and·water, so the medium must be sufficiently porous to allow atmospheric gases to diffuse through it, and to provide moisture without becoming waterlogged, or the roots will die.

The word 'compost' is used for the growing medium throughout the book. In small gardens, especially in towns, poor topsoil should almost certainly be replaced if possible with ready-mixed composts that include humus, fertilizers and drainage material. Pots, tubs and small beds will be packed with plants needing nourishment, so it is worth spending money on easily available commercial mixes.

Peat can be worked into small beds and containers. It retains moisture, helps the structure of the soil and increases acidity, but does not provide any food.

Surplus materials, including gravel, can be stored in large pots covered with lids, saucers or with other suitably shaped containers filled with plants. You could even conceal a hose pipe in this way.

Almost any bowl, tin or bucket can be used for plants provided that a drainage hole is made through the base, and provided the container is reasonably free from contamination. Paint containers of different shapes the same colour for a co-ordinated scheme.

Practical as well as aesthetic considerations are important when selecting containers. Even the best quality wood has a limited life if it is kept in close contact with the soil. Plastic tends to bow, buckle and discolour with use. Terracotta is vulnerable to frost damage in severe weather; and only the very best reconstituted stone containers will survive a knock from a car in your forecourt.

All container-grown plants need constant watering, but shallow pots dry out faster than deep ones. Narrow window boxes are unstable.

Opposite page: 1. Low-growing plants such as ivy. **2.** Saucer and plants can be lifted off to give access to: **3.** Bags of peat, etc

Above: 1. Plastic window box and tray in various colours; lengths from 15in. to 42in. (about 38cm to just over a metre); widths in proportion. **2.** Terracotta pots, diameters up to 18in. (about 45cm). **3.** Classic, ornamental pot. **4.** Patterned trough in reconstituted stone or terracotta. **5.** Stone jardinière. **6.** Container for herbs. **7.** Terracotta wall pots; the larger one stands on the ground, the two smaller ones are suspended on wall nails. **8.** Patterned and plain urns, derived from oil jars.

FEEDING

In many gardens the soil will have been cultivated for decades, plants will have extracted all useful foods – and pollution may have added unwanted soot and chemicals. It is therefore essential to make sure the soil is well balanced.

The addition of bulky, organic materials like peat or rotted manure will help to improve its structure and hold moisture. A long-term, slow-release organic fertilizer, which provides an even release of fertilizer to the soil for up to three months, can be used at twice the normal rate of 2oz per square yard (about 68gm per square metre) – after all, you will be asking a lot of your tiny garden.

Only localized soil improvement where you want to infiltrate new specimens will be necessary in established gardens – but remember to dig out all old roots and deep-rooted weeds when preparing positions for new plants.

It is best to buy fresh, specially prepared compost for window boxes and other containers. Garden soil can be used for these, if necessary, but be sure to remove large stones, weeds, etc. – and add peat and a good handful of organic fertilizer for every bucketful of soil. Remember, too, that this soil will be unsterilized and could carry pests and diseases that may occasionally affect seedlings or newly established plants. In addition you may well find that some of the tub plants (rhododendrons, azaleas, heaths, etc.) are lime-haters and require an acid growing medium.

There are five basic methods of feeding plants once they are growing:

1. Applying fertilizer to the surface of the soil around the base of the plant. Fertilizers are often formulated to achieve specific results – those for roses or tomatoes, for example, are high in potash to induce flowers or fruit. Follow manufacturers' instructions when applying fertilizers.

2. Mulching with organic, food-containing material, or with material combined with fertilizer. This feeds plants and also helps to maintain moisture and stifle weeds. All plants benefit, particularly surface-rooting types such as rhododendrons, camellias and azaleas. Feed them immediately after flowering in late spring or early summer – and remember to flood the root area first so that the subsequent mulch conserves the maximum amount of moisture.

3. Liquid fertilizers are particularly appropriate to tiny gardens. Easily mixed and watered on, they are ideal for window boxes and other containers where plants have matured and need feeding but where there is insufficient space for traditional fertilizers or mulching. It is essential to ensure that the soil is really moist before the fertilizer is applied.

4. Foliar feeds are absorbed through the plant's foliage, and the response in most cases is rapid.

5. Feeding-spikes are specially formulated to suit all kinds of plants from trees and shrubs to indoor specimens. Just push the spike into the soil among the plant's root system; water dry soil to help the spike start work.

Watering

Watering is the key to success in intensive gardening, both when growing new plants and when achieving performance from established ones bought from a garden store or nursery.

Established plants will have been accustomed to receiving their optimum water requirements, and during the first weeks in your garden they will have to be weaned away from this high water level. This generally means providing extra water initially, and reducing the amount systematically once the plant is established. It is vital to understand this concept. Plants like geraniums, for example, which will eventually tolerate hot, dry conditions, urgently need the maximum amount of water when they are first planted out or transferred to your own pots or tubs.

In open borders it is essential to ensure adequate moisture for the roots, and all established plants will benefit when their foliage is sprayed. The same rule applies to plants in containers, but there is an additional factor. If you allow a container to become too dry the soil or compost shrinks away from the sides, and water will run through this space, leaving a dry root ball. Always remember to break up the soil surface and introduce the water gradually so that it penetrates the centre of the ball.

There are no hard and fast rules for watering. However, the vast majority of people don't apply nearly enough water.

Particular care must be taken when establishing climbing plants or wall shrubs. The first 12in. (30cm) of soil next to a wall or fence always remains dry, so plants should be situated at least 9in. (23cm) inside the border or bed. Make sure the plants are well watered at the roots in the early stages – and spray foliage and shoots, particularly of self-clinging types.

PROPAGATION

Seeds

Although most commonly cultivated plants are represented in the lists of speciality seed houses, most people concentrate on annuals and other summer bedding plants and, possibly, biennials like wallflowers.

The summer plants include the half-hardy petunias, lobelia, marigolds and the recently introduced F^1 hybrid pelargoniums (geraniums), all of which can be sown towards the end of winter. Use sterilized compost, and fit small, plastic propagating cases onto the seed trays. Keep them as warm as possible until germination occurs.

When the seedlings show two leaves, prick them out into trays of compost (allowing about 1½in. – 4cm – between plants), or into proprietary peat cubes which give each seedling its own home. Always grasp a seedling by one of its leaves when pricking out – it doesn't matter if the leaf dies, but if the stem is infected by touching you lose the complete plant.

Leave the seedlings to grow in light, cool conditions until mid-spring, when the seed trays can be placed in a sheltered position outside. Cover them with glass or clear plastic until all risk of frost has passed.

Once the seedlings have been hardened off in this way, they can be planted outside, in late spring or early summer.

Geraniums (zonal pelargoniums) will grow at a faster rate if they are potted out into 3in. (about 7.5cm) pots filled with a

peat- or soil-based compost, and kept indoors in a very light position or under glass for a few weeks.

Wallflowers, sweet Williams, Canterbury bells and other biennials are sown in a warm spot in the border in mid-summer or in a seed tray. About a month later they can be transferred to other spaces to grow, then moved to their final positions in mid-autumn for flowering the following year.

Cuttings

Take cutting of half-hardy perennials such as fuchsias, *Helichrysum*, etc, in late summer. Select a non-flowering shoot and cut it off just below a leaf joint with a sharp knife or razor blade. Strip off the lower leaves, dip the cut end in hormone rooting powder and tap off the excess powder. Put in a tray or pot of sterile compost. Leave cuttings until they have rooted, then pot individually and keep throughout winter in light, frost-free conditions. Put them outside in mid-spring to harden off.

Layering and division

Layering, the simplest of all methods of propagation, consists of pegging long shoots of plants like periwinkles and some shrubs into the ground and covering them with soil; roots will be made at that point. Division is basically splitting up clumps of roots once a plant has been established for two or three years; this increases the number of plants, and also ensures strong growth from each new unit.

Top: To take cuttings from half-hardy perennials, cut with a sharp knife or razor blade just below a leaf joint **(1)**; remove leaves **(2, 3)**, dip cut end in hormone rooting powder, and insert cutting in compost (up to **4**). Cuttings are around the edge of the pot for additional air and better drainage.
Centre: Plastic propagation tray; the clear acrylic dome has two air vents. **Left:** Pot of seedlings protected by a clear plastic dome. The propagating tray contains peat-fibre pots, some with pricked-out seedlings.

GREENHOUSES

Any conventional greenhouse will take up too much of the limited space available in a tiny garden, and you will therefore probably be restricted to the narrow 'lean-to' type illustrated.

An aspect facing the rising or setting sun is best. A greenhouse in full sun will become very hot in summer, while a shaded one offers little advantage to plants other than frost protection during winter. Good light is vital for conventional crops.

Heating: Enough warmth to keep the greenhouse frost-free is necessary if you want to keep cuttings during winter. Electric heaters – tubular or fan type – are convenient and can be thermostatically controlled. Oil heaters are much less expensive, but can be messy and smelly.

Ventilation: The temperature rises rapidly in sunlight, even in early spring. Without an automatic ventilating system someone will have to be constantly on hand to open ventilators or doors. There are two systems: a device, activated by a change in temperature, that raises or lowers the conventional ventilation panel in the roof; and a small fan linked to a thermostatic switch.

Shading: This is vital during summer. Use exterior blinds, or specially formulated shading paint which can be removed if necessary in early winter.

Other considerations also have to be taken into account. Hot, dry conditions during summer encourage that doyenne of pests, the red spider mite – the most difficult for amateurs to detect and eradicate. Use two or three of the many insecticides available, in rotation, so that the mites have less chance to build up resistance to a single product.

Once a year during mild weather take all plants, containers, soil, etc. out of the greenhouse and clean and sterilize the framework, shelves and benches.

Automatic irrigation, once the prerogative of commercial growers, is now also available to amateurs. All systems are based on the principle of small quantities of water being released to give uniform coverage. However, the way in which the source of the water is controlled is more sophisticated and expensive in some systems than in others.

Lean-to greenhouse; sliding doors are an advantage where space is limited.

STRUCTURAL ADDITIONS AND CHANGES

Few people are lucky enough to inherit a garden that exactly reflects their vision of perfection. This section lists some materials that can be used to change its appearance and atmosphere, and describes some basic structural additions for your garden.

More major alterations like building walls and raised brick beds should only be undertaken by the truly competent amateur.

Materials

Bricks: These are available in a wide range of colours and finishes. It may occasionally be possible to find ones that match the house and garden walls but, even if not, most bricks eventually develop a mature look. Don't use really soft bricks for paving; water and frost will gradually cause their surface to flake. Demolition sites are useful sources for old, mature bricks.

Natural stone: The price of this material has rocketed in recent years. 'Crazy paving' – irregular shapes laid together with tight joints – produces an attractive effect but is best left to a skilled mason. Rectangular York paving is ideal with its controlled lines and subtle variations of colour that can only occur in a natural material; but it becomes extremely slippery in a shaded patio. Natural stone can be used for walls.

Artificial stones: These range from slabs made with natural aggregates to ones formed from coloured concrete. Surface textures vary, and some even have artificial depressions like those found in natural stone. Smaller slabs are useful in tiny areas, where their scale is preferable to standard sizes. Some coloured slabs fade quite quickly.

Matching artificial walling is available.

Tiles: Suitable for roof gardens as well as patios, most tiles are relatively thin and must be laid on a proper concrete base. Only use frost-resistant tiles outdoors, and be wary of glazed or highly polished products which can be very slippery when wet. Tiles should be laid by a professional.

Timber: This very adaptable material can be used to construct raised planters, as 'duck boarding' to provide sitting areas, and for balcony flooring.

Cedar is ideal for planters but expensive. However, it is too soft for flooring. Use a heavily preserved softwood for this.

Pools and Pumps

Glass fibre pool shells and less expensive plastic liners are easy to install, even for amateurs. Geometric shapes are well suited to town gardens.

Pumps re-circulate water, operating a fountain or some other water display. All that is necessary is a convenient electrical point with a weatherproof outlet; no external plumbing is needed. The cost of a pump increases in direct ratio to the volume of water it pumps, but it is worth remembering that while you can reduce the flow on a larger pump, you cannot increase it on a

Brickwork patterns include herringbone **(above)** and basketwork **(below)**.

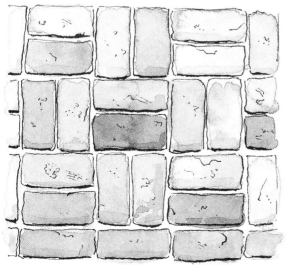

smaller one – and may be saddled with a disappointing display.

Trellis work and fencing
There is little to choose between the many proprietary trellis work panels on the market. Some units are too light to be self-supporting and are only suitable for decoration, or training plants to a wall. A ten-year-old climbing rose can be extremely heavy and also creates wind-resistance, so buy a panel that will be strong and secure for this purpose. An expandable trellis, opened fractionally to produce a pattern of elongated diamond shapes, creates an effective free-standing screen if it is framed by a plant that provides the necessary support and disguises its pointed ends.

Proprietary, expandable trellis in a softwood frame forms a free-standing screen. The detail shows: **1.** Capping about 3in. wide by ½in. deep (75mm by 12mm). **2.** Cover. **3.** Frame. **4.** Trellis.

SPECIAL PROJECTS

Small herb garden
A formal herb garden can be based on rectangles, diamonds or the Greek key pattern, as well as the squares shown here. Whatever shapes you choose, try to use complete bricks – avoid cutting them, if possible. The beds can be redivided into smaller units containing herbs.

Once you have decided on the pattern, mark out the paths, excavate the soil to a suitable level (using it for adjacent beds), and fill the base with hardcore or other material as a firm base for the bricks. These are bedded in sand or set in cement.

Edge the central beds with thyme, and plant angelica, dill, sweet fennel, rosemary, etc. in the perimeter borders for a more informal effect. A picket fence, or formal hedge, provides the finishing touch.

Alpine sink
The sink can be made of original stone (not easily available), reproduction stone or white, glazed china treated with cement slurry to give a rustic effect. Incorporate about 20% peat and soluble glue in the cement mix, and ensure adhesion by painting a coat of glue onto the sink beforehand.

Make sure there is adequate drainage – a layer of stones or broken pots. Compost should be free-draining, with 25% extra grit or coarse sand added to standard mixes.

Choose plants with complementary or contrasting foliage patterns and flower colours. Space is restricted, so select varieties that will remain reasonably compact: less invasive *sedums* and saxifrages are very suitable. Chippings cover the soil surface between plants.

Pieces of weathered rock can be arranged to form two or three 'outcrops'; put some plants in the crevices between the rocks.

Small-scale rockeries
Rocks of the neighbourhood are usually the most effective in rockeries, although lightweight, man-made stones are also available. In either case, keep their strata running horizontally and try to imagine how they would look in a natural setting.

Always build the rockery up from a sound base, adding soil to the pockets between the stones. Never try to cover a soil mound with rocks; and never build a rockery against house walls. Use good-quality plants – alpines, small conifers, Japanese maples, and miniature rhododendrons and azaleas, with alpine plants in crevices.

Raised sand pit. It can later be converted into a paddling pool.

Sand pit

Conventional sunken sand pits are easily contaminated – and often used by local cats. A raised box like the one illustrated is easily covered and cleaned out.

It consists of two basic sections: a shallow box, 6in. (15cm) deep, with a narrow seat around the inner edge; and a lightweight, plywood cover, slightly wider and longer than the box.

Formal herb garden.

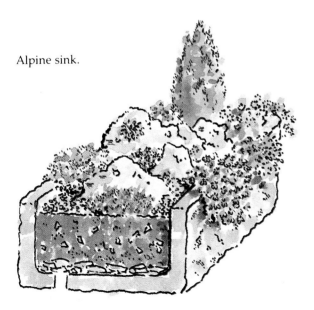

Alpine sink.

Rockery.

FRONT DOORS
AND ENTRANCES

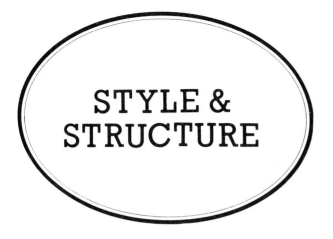

STYLE & STRUCTURE

The architectural style and balance of a doorway obviously dictate how containers are arranged, what plants you choose, and where you put them – depending, of course, on personal taste and available space. Classic entrances should generally be treated simply and symmetrically – a pair of bay trees is often all that is needed. Other doorways may call for an asymmetrical design.

However, it is almost more important to select containers and plants that are in keeping with the style of the doorway: traditional clay pots or wooden tubs planted with soft, tumbling foliage for cottages; smart modern cylinders holding sculptural plants for contemporary houses.

It is often possible to transform a simple container by adding a little moulding or other architectural embellishment that reflects decorative details on the doorway. Or paint it in a colour that complements or contrasts with the walls.

If you live in an area where there is a risk of vandalism, chain tubs to adjacent rails or surrounds, and cement stone containers to the ground – always making sure that the drainage hole remains unobstructed. In either case, avoid long-stemmed or easily broken plants.

When placing large containers against house walls, always leave enough space to

Left: The shrubs and their square containers complement the formal front door and the angles made by the iron railings.

Panelled door with fanlight. Match its classic style with carefully shaped shrubs and climbers.

Door with stained-glass panels. Secure containers to the steps if there is a risk of vandalism.

Modern glass doors with shutters. Outside paving provides good drainage for pots and tubs.

Modern front door with paved front yard. Use taller plants for framing, and to soften its angles.

keep the gap free of leaves, compost and rubbish that would otherwise build up and cause dampness in the wall.

If climbing plants are to be encouraged onto the façade of the house or over surrounding railings, always try to plant them directly into the soil, even if this means removing paving or concrete. Plants in containers will never be able to achieve their full growth and luxuriant effect.

Dryness can be a problem when doorways are in full sun. To provide moisture put saucers of water underneath pots and keep them full during hot months.

GREEN SKELETON

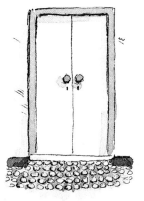

Modern door. To complement its simple style, combine a neat, bold planting with striking containers.

Cottage door. Match its character with climbing roses, creepers and well-filled tubs of flowers.

Sun

1. Brightly coloured ivy, *Hedera helix* 'Jubilee'. **2.** Summer-flowering jasmine, *Jasminum officinale*. **3.** Climbing rose; possibilities include cream-white 'Handel' and silvery-pink 'New Dawn'. **4.** The mop-headed bay tree, *Laurus nobilis*, is immediately effective. Trim the new growth in late spring and spray at fortnightly intervals during summer with a systemic insecticide. A gum tree, *Eucalyptus gunnii*, would be an informally shaped alternative. It can be cut back each year to encourage new, soft grey foliage. **5.** *Yucca filamentosa*. The following plants, each with their own form, contribute interesting foliage and, with the exception of spring-flowering rosemary, bloom in summer: **6.** Rosemary, *Rosmarinus officinalis* and *Cotoneaster conspicuus* 'Decorus'; **7.** Grey-leaved *Senecio greyi*; **8.** Lavender, *Lavandula*. **9.** The African lily, *Agapanthus*, has bright green strap-like foliage and blue flower spikes in summer. Use seasonal and rockery plants to soften the edges of flower pots and borders.

19th-century style door, ideal for plants in pots or tubs. The iron railings are an attractive feature.

Shade

1. The climbing rose 'Mermaid' keeps its leaves and single cream-yellow flowers into winter. Its colour is picked up by: **2.** The large-leaved golden ivy, *Hedera colchica dentata* 'Aurea'. **3.** Winter jasmine, *Jasminum nudiflorum*. **4.** *Mahonia japonica*, another winter-flowering shrub, has an interesting foliage pattern. **5.** *Viburnum tinus* 'Eve Price' gives yet more winter interest, with blush-pink flowers that contrast with its sea-green foliage. Devote some space to plants which lie dormant in winter: **6.** Hardy ferns like *Asplenium*, *Phyllitis* and *Pteridium*; and **7.** Plantain lilies, *Hosta*.

Small-leaved ivies like *Hedera helix* 'Glacier' and *H. helix* 'Sagittaefolia' soften the edges of pots, and the earth.

Sun

Shade

SPRING

At your front door, more than anywhere else, you will be aware of the first movement of foliage, the first flowers of spring. Whatever all-year treatment you adopt, be sure to include some plants – permanent or otherwise – that will provide colour and greenery early in the season.

This is the ideal spot to experiment with small groupings of bulbs, and decide which of the many species, colours and sizes appeal to you. Select them carefully to create continuous splashes of colour from the first weeks of spring.

Introduce forced plants – polyanthus, cinerarias, calceolarias, primulas – to flower in late spring before half-hardy plants are installed for summer. Space for seasonal plants is restricted, so it should not be an expensive operation.

Sun: 1. Golden honeysuckle, *Lonicera japonica* 'Aureoreticulata'. Plant direct in ground. **2.** Low troughs contain polyanthus, *Primula polyantha*, mixed with tulips 'Bellona'. **3.** The flax, *Phormium tenax* 'tricolor', holds its shape all year round. **4.** A gum tree, *Eucalyptus gunnii.* Cut back to provide new growth. **5.** A dwarf broom, *Genista lydia*; its bright green stems bear golden-yellow flowers. **6.** The climbing rose 'Mrs. Sam McCredy'. Plant direct in ground. **7.** Lavender, *Lavandula* 'Hidcote'. **8.** *Hebe* 'Bowles Variety'. A light trim will keep it in shape for summer. **9.** Narcissi 'Ice Follies'.

Spring only: 1. Japanese quince, *Chaenomeles speciosa* or *C. japonica*, flowers before its leaves appear. **2.** Clematis, *C. montana.* 'Alba' has white flowers, 'Rubens' has pink ones, both in late spring. Prune after flowering. **3.** The camellia, *C.* x *williamsii* 'Donation', is an evergreen and bears single, pink flowers with yellow centres. **4.** Single, blue anemones, *A. hepatica.* **5.** Pale and dark blue pansies, *Viola* x *wittrockiana*, interplanted with white narcissi with orange trumpets, 'Geranium'. **6.** Rosemary, *Rosmarinus officinalis* 'Jessop's Upright', has blue flowers in early spring. **7.** The hellebore, *Helleborus corsicus*, bears greeny-white flowers before its foliage appears.

Shade: 1. The Mexican mock orange, *Choisya ternata*, has bright, evergreen foliage. **2.** The low bowl contains short, multi-head tulips, *Tulipa praestans* 'Fusilier,' inter-planted with forget-me-nots, *Myosotis.* **3.** *Bergenia* 'Silberlicht' has bold foliage with silvery-pink flowers in early spring. **4.** The climbing rose 'Mermaid' is a dormant tracery. **5.** The hydrangea, *H.* 'Blue Wave', is dormant. **6.** Vase with mid-season narcissi to choice. **7.** *Garrya elliptica*; its evergreen foliage has the added bonus of long 'catkins' through early spring.

Sun: 1. The common myrtle, *Myrtus communis*, is a good, year-round evergreen. **2.** Half-pots or other low containers house crocuses; replace these with polyanthus, *Primula polyantha*—or other forced plants—before summer. **3.** *Caryopteris* x *clandonensis.* Cut back to promote growth. **4.** Cineraria, *C. maritima* 'White Diamond' has silver, velvety leaves. **5.** *Hebe carnosula* has small, silver-green leaves. **6.** The clematis, *C. armandii*, has evergreen foliage and small, white, waxen flowers. **7.** Day lilies, *Hemerocallis.* **8.** *Sedum* x 'Autumn Joy' emerges after winter. Large pots are edged with *Aubretia*; bellflowers, *Campanula*; and candytuft, *Iberis.*

Conifers: 1. The cypresses, *Chamaecyparis lawsoniana* 'Erecta', have bright green, even growth. **2.** The pine, *Pinus mugo*, is interestingly shaped and remains compact. **3.** The juniper, *Juniperus horizontalis*, is low and spreading. **4.** *Thuja occidentalis* 'Rheingold' forms a mound of golden foliage. **5.** The Japanese cedar, *Cryptomeria japonica*, has bronze-tinted foliage. **6.** Another juniper, *J.* 'Pfitzerana', is of horizontal habit with spreading and arching branches.

Shade: 1. Golden Irish yew, *Taxus baccata* 'Fastigiata Aurea'. **2.** Spotted laurel, *Aucuba crotonifolia.* **3.** Seasonal planting of white hyacinths edged with dormant ferns. **4.** Seasonal planting of cream and pale pink narcissi 'Mrs. R. O. Backhouse'. **5.** Firethorns, *Pyracantha,* are clipped to repeat the stark form of the doorway. **6.** Plantain lily, *Hosta glauca*; its foliage is only just emerging. **7.** Tough but fragile-appearing *Helxine soleirolii* is planted between cobbles and allowed to run around the bases of the pots. The edges of the pots containing **1** and **4** are softened with variegated ivy, *Hedera helix* 'Glacier'.

Roses: 1. White, climbing rose 'Wedding Day'. **2.** Clear pink, climbing rose 'Aloha'. **3.** Pink-shaded apricot, standard roses 'Silver Jubilee'. **4.** Cerise-flushed scarlet, half-standard roses 'Wendy Cussons'. **5.** Brilliant red, bush roses 'Alec's Red'. Colours in **3, 4** and **5** graduate from pale to deep. **6.** Edging of lavender, *Lavandula* 'Munstead', or box, *Buxus.*

SUMMER

Thorough watering is essential in any part of the garden during summer – and especially so at front doors. Even during rainy periods most plants will remain dry in the lee of the house wall, especially if they are in containers. Natural rainfall will not provide sufficient moisture – water is either prevented from settling on the plants, or the leaves 'bounce' raindrops away from root areas.

Heavy watering at least once a week is a must – unless the doorway is in a really shaded position or the rain has been truly torrential. Where possible, stand containers on saucers to conserve water during hot, dry spells.

Install half-hardy seasonal plants, for summer flowering, as soon as the last frost has passed.

Sun: 1. Golden honeysuckle. **2.** Troughs are planted with white, single geraniums (zonal pelargoniums) and warm pink petunias. **3.** Flax. **4.** There is new, bright silver growth on the gum tree. **5.** Trim back the broom immediately after flowering. **6.** The climbing rose 'Mrs. Sam McCredy' is in flower. **7.** The lavender starts to flower in late summer. **8.** *Hebe.* **9.** White tobacco plants, *Nicotiana affinis*, provide evening scent and are supported by other plants.

Summer only: 1. Plume poppy, *Macleaya cordata*; its leaves have silver undersides and it bears coral flowers. **2.** The rambling rose 'Albertine' has only one flush of flower, but there is nothing to equal its subtle apricot-pink colour. **3.** Fig, *Ficus carica* 'Brown Turkey'. On a sunny wall there may even be some fruit. **4.** Dark blue bedding lobelia forms a carpet of colour. **5.** Geraniums (zonal pelargoniums) in the colour of your choice. **6.** *Potentilla fruticosa*. **7.** The irises, *I. sibirica* 'Snow Queen', have small, white flowers and fine, strap-like leaves.

Shade: 1. The Mexican mock orange has an abundance of white, star-like flowers in early summer. Trim immediately after flowering to retain overall form. **2.** Planting of pale pink busy Lizzie, *Impatiens sultanii*. **3.** *Bergenia.* **4.** Large, cream, single roses with sulphur centres are produced against dark green foliage. **5.** The hydrangea is in full foliage with green and white variegated leaves. **6.** Deep scarlet tobacco plants, *Nicotiana* 'Crimson Bedder', are edged with pale blue, trailing lobelia. **7.** *Garrya.*

SPECIAL

Sun: 1. The myrtle has white flowers in mid- and late summer. **2.** Half-pots are filled with 'multiflora' begonias in orange, red or yellow. **3.** *Caryopteris*; light green leaves precede pale blue flowers. **4.** The cineraria grows strongly with yellow flowers in mid-summer. **5.** The *Hebe* is covered in small, white, cone-shaped flowers in late summer. **6.** The clematis retains its shape. It is important to keep it moist through summer. **7.** The day lilies have lush foliage and 'one day only' flowers. **8.** The *Sedum* is in full foliage.

Useful: 1. Loganberry, *Rubus* x *loganobaccus*. **2.** Fan-trained peach, *Prunus persica*, underplanted with Alpine strawberries 'Baron Solemacher'. **3.** Strawberry pot planted with strawberries of your choice. **4.** Runner beans. **5.** Parsley. **6.** Rosemary, *Rosmarinus officinalis*. **7.** Mint. **8.** Tomato; 'Amateur' needs no staking.

Shade: 1. Yew. **2.** Spotted laurel. Cut back its branches occasionally to keep compact growth. **3.** Seasonal planting of white busy Lizzie, *Impatiens sultanii*. Ferns have put on summer growth. **4.** Seasonal planting of half-hardy pale pink and white fuchsias, including trailing varieties to tumble down the side of the container. These could include 'Pink Fairy' and 'White Spider'. **5.** Keep the firethorns' new growth clipped back to ensure short flowering stems and berries. **6.** The plantain lily is in full leaf. **7.** The *Helxine* spreads rapidly while the days are warm.

For the blind: 1. The jasmine, *Jasminum officinale*, has perfumed flowers throughout summer and needs no training. **2.** The clematis, *C. tangutica*, has silken seed heads. Lavender, *Lavandula*, at its base bears fragrant flowers in summer. **3.** The magnolia, *M. grandiflora*, bears perfumed flowers in summer. **4.** *Mahonia japonica* has scented flowers from mid-winter to spring. **5.** *Daphne odora* bears perfumed flowers. The sun rose, *Cistus*, has aromatic leaves. **6.** Seasonal plantings: mignonette for summer; hyacinths for spring. **7.** Raised bed for aromatic herbs.

AUTUMN

Autumn colour derives from many sources. Some seasonal plants like busy Lizzie flourish until the first frost, while half-hardy perennials such as geraniums and marguerites can be nursed along until well into the season. Late-flowering herbaceous plants, and shrubs like fuchsias and hydrangeas, will also continue to provide colour. Hydrangeas in particular produce flowers in late summer which age gracefully during the following weeks.

Japanese maples display stunning autumn tints and come in a diverse range of growth patterns which makes it easy to fit one of these shrubs into almost any scheme. Brilliant colour also comes from the self-clinging Virginia creeper.

Berried plants add further interest, but only briefly – they are all too often stripped by birds.

Sun: 1. Honeysuckle. **2.** The petunias have probably finished, but the geraniums continue into autumn. **3.** Flax. **4.** The gum tree's growth slows as days become cooler. **5.** Broom. **6.** Long branches on the rose are 'arched' over, shortened and tied in. **7.** The lavender continues to flower; 'Hidcote' is a particularly rich colour. **8.** The *Hebe* is covered in pale mauve flowers; greeny-purple leaves make a perfect foil. **9.** Side shoots will follow on if original flowers are removed from the tobacco plants.

Autumn only: 1. The white-flowered variety of hydrangea blooms from late summer through autumn. **2.** *Cotoneaster* x *rothschildianus* has creamy-yellow berries. **3.** Korean-type chrysanthemums planted in early summer. **4.** The Virginia creeper, *Parthenocissus*, is a mass of red and orange tones. **5.** *Fatsia japonica* has cream plumes on top of large, evergreen leaves. **6.** Dwarf Michaelmas daisies, *Aster alpinus*, provide useful colour. **7.** The Japanese maple, *Acer palmatum* 'Dissectum', displays a fantastic range of colours as its leaves turn.

Shade: 1. Mexican mock orange. **2.** Busy Lizzie, grown to huge proportions, will collapse at the first frost. **3.** *Bergenia*. **4.** The rose produces long growths which should be tied in or removed. Its thorns are particularly vicious, so keep the doorway clear. **5.** The hydrangea is in full flower. **6.** The tobacco plants remain in flower and may need subtle staking with small, branched twigs. The lobelia has probably finished. **7.** *Garrya*.

Sun 1. Myrtle. **2.** The begonias continue to flower. **3.** The *Caryopteris* is in full flower until the first frost. **4.** The cineraria keeps its bright silver foliage. **5.** *Hebe.* **6.** Clematis. **7.** Day lilies. **8.** The *Sedum* has a profusion of crimson/maroon, flat flower heads.

Low maintenance/shade: 1. The hydrangeas, *H. petiolaris*, are slow-growing and self-clinging, with symmetrical heads of white flowers in summer. **2.** *Viburnum tinus*; evergreen, the bushes have small, pink and white flowers in winter, followed by blue-black berries. **3.** Vases planted with *Lonicera pileata*. **4.** Underplantings of blue periwinkle, *Vinca minor*.

Shade: 1. Yew. **2.** The spotted laurel sometimes carries amber/red fruit. **3.** Remove busy Lizzies and replace with dwarf, pink or crimson chrysanthemums bought in flower from a florist. **4.** Fuchsias should continue to flower well into autumn. **5.** The firethorns have red or orange fruit depending on variety. **6.** Plantain lily. **7.** *Helxine.*

Low maintenance/sun: 1. Virginia creeper, *Ampelopsis* 'Beverly Brook', produces attractively coloured leaves in autumn. **2.** *Viburnum rhytidophyllum* has white flowers in late spring. **3.** The crimson buds of the sun roses, *Cistus* x *corbariensis*, open to white in early summer. **4.** Spanish gorse, *Genista hispanica*, has yellow flowers in late spring.

Overleaf: The clean lines of the cast-stone containers are offset by the soft foliage of fuchsias, geraniums and lobelia.

WINTER

Investment in evergreen shrubs pays dividends during the winter. The foliage of each specimen is different, often contrasting with the gaunt skeletons of deciduous plants and adding interest throughout the season.

Most herbaceous plants die back – *Bergenia*, which maintains its leathery leaves, is an exception; and seasonal plants offer a limited range of colour. Only winter cherries provide a bright display. Most space will be given over to dormant bulbs and to uninteresting foliage that will blossom forth in the spring.

It is vital to check plants for dryness during mild spells, and water them if necessary. Because they do not transpire on colder, and often wetter, days it will not be apparent that they are drying out at the roots. When the first warm days of spring arrive and water is demanded, plants will suffer dramatically if it is not available.

Sun: 1. The honeysuckle keeps most of its leaves in a mild winter. **2.** Troughs are planted with forget-me-nots, *Myosotis*; and scarlet tulips, *Tulipa eichleri*. **3.** Flax. **4.** The gum tree provides grey foliage throughout winter. **5.** *Genista*. **6.** The rose is dormant. **7.** Lavender, and **8.** *Hebe* give soft winter form. **9.** Narcissi 'Mount Hood' are planted among the shrubs.

Winter only: 1. The ornamental cherry, *Prunus subhirtella* 'Autumnalis Rosea', carries pale pink flowers intermittently from mid-autumn to early spring. **2.** Ivy, *Hedera helix* 'Sagittaefolia'; its small, dark green leaves are a perfect foil for the cherry. **3.** Another ivy, *H.h.* 'Jubilee', has small, bright yellow and green leaves. **4.** The Chinese witch hazel, *Hamamelis mollis*, provides yellow flowers on bare stems. **5.** The rhododendron, *R.* 'Praecox', has pale mauve flowers and is one of the first to flower. **6.** The Christmas rose, *Helleborus niger*. **7.** The architectural form of the cabbage palm, *Cordyline indivisa*, is perfect for a container.

Shade: 1. Mexican mock orange. **2.** Planting of polyanthus, *Primula polyantha*; and crocuses. **3.** The first flowers appear on the *Bergenia* in late winter. **4.** The rose carries its foliage and the occasional flower into early winter. **5.** The hydrangea has shed its leaves, but dried flowers remain. **6.** Vase planted with early narcissi 'Peeping Tom' with winter cherries, *Solanum capsicastrum*, above for early winter colour. **7.** The *Garrya* shows its first few catkins.

Sun: 1. The myrtle retains its glossy, dark green foliage. **2.** Half-pots are filled with early narcissi, 'February Gold'. Winter cherries, *Solanum capsicastrum*, are planted on the surface above them, and removed as the bulbs appear in early spring. **3.** The blue flowers of the *Caryopteris* have dried to golden-brown. **4.** Trim the cineraria to encourage neat form. **5.** *Hebe*. **6.** Clematis. **7.** Keep the day lilies tidy as foliage dies. **8.** The dry flower heads on the *Sedum* can remain—or use them to make an attractive indoor arrangement. Remove foliage as it dies back.

Shade: 1. Yew. **2.** Spotted laurel. **3.** Planting of narcissi, 'W. P. Milner'. **4.** Plant vase with mixed wallflowers, *Cheiranthus*, interplanted with cream or lemon yellow, single, mid-season tulips. **5.** The firethorns should hold most of their leaves through winter. **6.** The plantain lily is dormant. **7.** *Helxine* deteriorates during winter; keep tidy, ready for spring growth.

SPECIAL

Formal: This simple, classic style is easy to maintain. Remember to leave a narrow margin of space all round tubs or pots; and buy trees that are – and will remain – in the right proportion for the containers.

Bay trees, *Laurus nobilis*, can be used in the following shapes: pyramid, standard or mop head, half standard, bush.

Box, *Buxus*, can be shaped **(left)** to form a spiral, pyramid or ball. Suitable conifers include *Chamaecyparis lawsoniana* 'Ellwoodii'; holly, *Ilex* 'Pyramidalis'; common yew, *Taxus baccata*, trimmed to shape

Climbing plants trained over pyramid **(left)** or obelisk supports made from softwood frames filled in with expandable trellis achieve an effect similar to shaped trees.

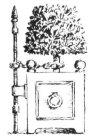

To secure trees against vandals, wrap a steel chain around the base of each tree and the railing; and fix a rigid bracket to the side of the box and around the railing.

COVERED PORCHES

In all but the warmest climates, porches are generally designed to protect house entrances from bad weather. When they are glazed to provide protection, they effectively become cold conservatories.

Early period houses frequently have verandahs running along the full face of the building. The main problem with these is lack of light, particularly when a solid roof only allows it to enter from the front. Shade-loving plants are essential under these circumstances, and even these will orientate themselves towards the light source.

Naturally, the deeper the verandah the greater the problem. For this reason a number of plans include furniture which will occupy space and provide interest throughout the year; brightly coloured cushions or table cloths, plant stands and wire jardinières can be added in summer.

Your choice of plants for the periphery of a porch or verandah is important. Blocks of taller evergreens can be placed at either end, giving a sense of enclosure. Climbing plants trained up the supports will soften – or disguise – them. Low plants at floor level help to link the building with the garden.

For total protection during winter, fix a series of simple, acrylic screens to the structural framework. This will allow you to keep citrus trees and other tender plants in a frost-free environment, with the occasional aid of a small fan-heater.

The most difficult technical problem is keeping the plants clean – no rain reaches them to wash off accumulations of dust and dirt. If they are in easily moved containers they can be taken into the garden and hosed down – or simply left outside during showers. Otherwise, you will have to clean each leaf individually, or use a fine spray of clear water to remove the dirt.

Summer/shade: 1. Lush evergreens embrace the porch. *Elaeagnus* x *ebbingei*, *Fatsia japonica* and *Hydrangea villosa* are all suitable. **2.** Ivy, *Hedera helix* 'Goldheart', is trained onto step risers. **3.** Shade-tolerant ferns and other foliage plants in containers and on raised stand. Suggestions include: *Nephrolepsis*; *Chlorophytum*; pale lime-green flame nettles, *Coleus*; and bellflowers, *Campanula isophylla*. **4.** Narrow window boxes on the wooden balustrade hold ivy, *Hedera helix* 'Herald'; *Asparagus sprengeri*; and white and pale pink busy Lizzie, *Impatiens*. **5.** Hanging baskets or ceramic containers house shade-loving, trailing plants: ivy, including dark green *Hedera helix* 'Chicago'; trailing *Nepeta*; and trailing, half-hardy fuchsias, 'White Spider'. **6.** Large fern on table; *Asplenium* does well outside in summer, in a shady spot. **7.** Virginia creeper, *Parthenocissus quinquefolia*, planted outside the porch and trained along its top beam hangs down to form a foliage 'curtain'. **8.** House wall painted dark green; furniture and other woodwork is white, cushions are green.

Spring: 1. Climbing roses and clematis on vertical panels. Choose colours to complement or contrast with the paintwork: red 'Parkdirektor Riggers' roses and pale pink clematis, *C.* 'Hagley Hybrid', on white or cream woodwork; cream-yellow 'Mermaid', blush pink 'New Dawn' or pale apricot 'Lady Hillingdon' roses with white clematis, *C. armandii*, on black, dark green or grey paintwork. Both roses and deciduous clematis break into leaf; *C. armandii* bears white flowers. **2.** Substantial planting of evergreens – common laurel, *Prunus laurocerasus*, or yew, *Taxus* – form a screen throughout the year. **3.** Container planted with *Fatsia japonica* for year-round effect. Move it out and wash down every week. **4.** Low planting of box, *Buxus*, to disguise the base to the floor; clip it to complement the Regency architecture. **5.** Strands of green ivy, *Hedera*, from outside the porch are trained over the back wall. **6.** Wire jardinière or plant stand containing spring-flowering plants from other parts of the garden, or bought from a nursery. Include polyanthus, *Primula polyantha*; *P. obconica*; *Genista racemosa*; cineraria; and forced narcissi, crocuses and hyacinths. Small pots of trailing ivy soften the edges, and survive the gloomy situation.

Summer: 1. The climbing roses are in bloom, as is the summer-flowering clematis. **2.** Evergreens have a new flush of foliage. Trim as necessary. **3.** *Fatsia*. **4.** The box has new, pale green foliage. **5.** The ivy continues to grow. Trim as necessary. **6.** The jardinière or plant stand is filled with summer plants: fuchsias; busy Lizzie, *Impatiens*; half-hardy ferns, *Asparagus sprengeri*; and flame nettles, *Coleus*. *Primula obconica* flowers well into summer. **7.** Pots of standard fuchsias like 'Melody' and 'Cascade' give additional colour.

Enclosed porch/summer: 1. Corner unit – pot on a saucer, or a container with an automatic watering device – with a year-round, evergreen climbing plant: *Rhoicissus rhomboidea* or *Cissus antarctica* in milder areas; ivies like *Hedera canariensis* 'Gloire de Marengo', or plain green *Hedera helix* 'Chicago' where frosts are prevalent. The underplanting is *Fatsia japonica*. **2.** Corner unit has x *Fatshedera lizei* against the wall, underplanted with *Aspidistra*. **3.** Window boxes at sill level are planted with geraniums (zonal pelargoniums), regal pelargoniums and silver cineraria, *C. maritima*. **4.** Inner edges are covered by *Helichrysum petiolatum*. Morning glory, *Ipomoea*, is allowed to trail up around the edge of the glass frame, from the corners. **5.** Hanging baskets or ceramic planters hold trailing varieties of tuberous begonias; choose colours to co-ordinate with the plants in the window boxes.

Small, enclosed areas are particularly prone to attack by red spider mites, especially during summer. Spray at weekly intervals from the time you install the plants. Also during summer, damp the floor every day and leave the door open for ventilation.

Covered porch/summer: 1. A vine, *Vitis* 'Black Hambourg', planted outside in the border is trained along the wall into the porch. **2.** The jasmine, *Jasminum polyanthum*, bears sweetly scented white flowers from late spring to early summer. **3.** Pots of scented-leaf geraniums, *Pelargonium tomentosum*. **4.** Pots of African lilies, *Agapanthus*. **5.** Citrus trees – orange or lemon – in containers. **6.** The camellias, *C.* x *williamsii* 'J.C. Williams', have flowers with pink outer petals and sulphur centres from winter until mid-spring. **7.** The glass-roofed porch is transformed by cladding the supporting structure with pillars and arches of fine mesh trellis work. **8.** Seats are a feature in their own right. **9.** Statuette.

Fix panels of flat, clear acrylic sheeting into the archways during winter to protect the jasmine and citrus trees from frost, while enabling the vine to remain dormant. Potted camellias brought in from outside will produce early flowers from mid-winter onwards.

Autumn: 1. Climbing roses and clematis are in their last flush of flower. **2.** Evergreens. **3.** The *Fatsia* has white flowers in mid-autumn. **4.** Box. **5.** Ivy. **6.** Replace summer plants with chrysanthemums; the acid greens and yellows of the ferns complement their colours. **7.** Standard fuchsias give greenery if not flowers until late autumn when they must be moved to a frost-free area.

Winter: 1. Roses are dormant, although the rose 'Mermaid' has dark green foliage until mid-winter. Clematis often carries seed heads until well into winter. **2.** Evergreens. **3.** *Fatsia*; make sure the container does not dry out, and move out during mild, rainy weather. **4.** Box provides a splash of green during grey, winter months. **5.** Ivy; watch out for greenfly in this protected situation – new, young tips could be infested by the end of winter. **6.** Plants to provide colour until mid-winter include: Cape heather, *Erica gracilis*; winter cherries, *Solanum capsicastrum*; and ornamental peppers, *Capsicum frutescens*. All are available from garden centres. Replace ferns with pots of ivy. Plant bulbs in pots ready to bring them into the porch in spring. Any bulbs planted in pots on the porch itself will grow tall and weak, and collapse before they flower.

HANGING BASKETS

Above: A luxuriant basket in a blend of pinks: busy Lizzie, fuchsias and striped petunias. Established ivies provide long, green trails.

Far left: Bright pink geraniums and orange marigolds contrast with pale pink, trailing fuchsias and the soft blue haze of the lobelia.

Left: Terracotta pots, or plain pots in basketwork containers, can be hung from hooks or fixed to the walls.

Preparation: Hang the basket over a bench or table. **1.** Line it evenly with sphagnum moss, thick enough to retain compost. **2.** Prise the wire strands apart, and insert seedlings or small, pot-grown plants. **3.** Raise the compost level to cover the seedlings' roots.

4. Include larger, pot-grown plants in the final layer, covering the root balls with ½in. (1.25cm) of compost. The surface should be ½in. (1.25cm) below the basket rim.

STYLE & STRUCTURE

The tiniest of tiny gardens, hanging baskets filled with flowers, foliage or a mixture of both have great charm and provide decorative – and inexpensive – accents against walls and as part of overall plans for balconies, roof gardens and other areas.

The traditional wire baskets are usually lined with sphagnum moss, and both sides and tops can be planted to create colourful and imaginative effects. Remember, though, that because there is no surrounding humidity the compost will dry out faster than compost in boxes and borders – and that in summer a classic basket 'dripping' with colour will need to be watered daily. It is therefore vital that watering be made easy – devices for lowering or raising the basket, and for swivelling it to ensure even light, are available.

Don't stint on materials. Use fresh compost when the whole planting is renewed each year – and use the best you can find. It will have to support a massive network of roots during the growing period. Try to select well-formed, bushy plants.

In addition to wire baskets there is a wide range of containers including ceramic pots suspended in macramé, terracotta pots, pots in basketwork holders, and plastic bowls with integral saucers. All these take slightly longer to dry out than the baskets.

Ceramic container suspended in macramé; whole and half wire baskets. Secure all containers carefully.

SPRING

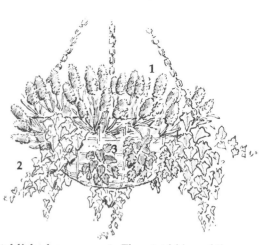

N̲o one has so far developed trailing bulbs, so the light, relaxed effect normally associated with hanging baskets has to be achieved with evergreen, over-wintering, trailing plants – usually one of the many small-leaved ivies.

Plant bulbs among these in autumn, to give a compact, colourful centre to the basket when flowers are produced in spring. Crocuses, grape hyacinths and short narcissi are all suitable, as are dwarf, multi-headed tulips and miniature irises.

A word of caution: the way bulbs perform is affected by the moisture content of the soil – dry patches lead to inconsistent flowering. It is vital to moisten baskets adequately before and after preparation – and to inspect them regularly, especially if they are under an overhang.

Established greenery: 1. The vivid blue of the grape hyacinths, *Muscari*, combines with: **2.** The grey of the variegated ivy, *Hedera helix* 'Glacier', and: **3.** The fresh, green leaves of the bellflowers, *Campanula garganica*.
   Note: There is a limit to where bulbs can be placed without disturbing the established planting.

SUMMER

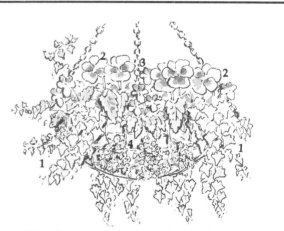

A̲ hanging basket can provide instant colour at eye-level. Carefully planted and well maintained, it will form a sphere of flowers and foliage. Use the best materials you can afford to create this effect, and take particular care with the planting.

Although it is unnecessary to use expensive specimens, the occasional well-grown fuchsia or geranium is immediately effective. There are endless combinations of plants; regard the basket as a clean canvas on which to paint as gaudy or subtle a picture as you wish.

Prepare baskets immediately after all danger of frost has passed – earlier if they can be hung under glass for a couple of weeks. Never allow them to dry out. This could mean watering them thoroughly every day, with liquid fertilizer applied at fortnightly intervals.

Established greenery: 1. The variegated ivy has a new flush of silvery-green leaves. Keep it well trimmed to encourage a bushy habit: remove the old growth on the underside of the plant, leaving the new growth. **2.** Plant garden pansies, *Viola* x *wittrockiana*, as soon as any bulbs finish. Choose from an extravagant array of colours—yellow and rust and purple—and team them with: **3.** Heartsease, *Viola tricolor*, as a contrast. **4.** The bellflowers produce blue blooms as the heartsease and pansies begin to fade.

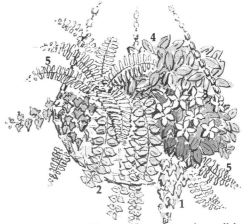

Bulbs: 1. Crocuses in mixed colours, planted both around the top perimeter and around the bowl of the basket. **2.** Short, multi-headed tulips, *Tulipa praestans* 'Fusilier'.

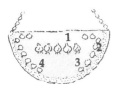

Planting plan: 1. Tulip bulbs; plant at a depth about 1½ times their height. **2.** Damp sphagnum moss. **3.** Crocus bulbs; space out horizontally to avoid vertical lines. **4.** Compost; put a thin layer between moss and bulbs.

Foliage/shade: 1. Choose a variety of small-leaved ivies, such as *Hedera helix* 'Discolor', *H. h.* 'Glacier', *H. h.* 'Goldheart', or *H. h.* 'Jubilee'. As trailing stems are produced peg them into the moss with small wire hoops until the underside of the basket is covered. **2.** Creeping Jenny, *Lysimachia nummularia*, has fresh green, tumbling foliage. **3.** The periwinkle, *Vinca minor*, has year-round foliage and pale blue flowers in late spring. **4.** Low-growing spotted laurel, *Aucuba japonica* 'Nana Rotundifolia', provides a foliage pattern to contrast with the trailing and tumbling plants. **5.** Ladder ferns—*Phyllitis, Pteridium* or *Asplenium*—can be set into the sides and top of the basket.

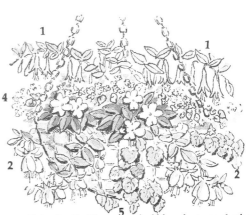

Massed effect: Select plants which will give the basket overall cover, both top and sides. Bellflowers, *Campanula isophylla*, are shown above.

For sunny positions try lobelias in either pale or dark blue, or mixed; alyssum, which will make a completely white basket; or marigolds, *Tagetes*, for a dazzling yellow/orange basket. In very full sun plant mesembryanthemums in vivid colours.

For shady positions try busy Lizzie, *Impatiens*; or a completely green or variegated ivy—variegations may vanish if there is not enough light.

In half-shade plant parsley or white or blue bellflowers, *Campanula isophylla*.

Seasonal/shade: 1. Choose a half-hardy type fuchsia of a colour to harmonize or contrast with: **2.** A trailing fuchsia of your choice; these are at their best in hanging baskets because you look up into the bell of the flower. **3.** A white busy Lizzie, *Impatiens sultanii*, around the edges and insides of the basket fills in any gaps between major plants. **4.** Small-flowered wax begonias, *B. semperflorens*, in cream or pale yellow to contrast with the pink and purple of the fuchsias. **5.** *Nepeta hederacea* 'Variegata' is a trailing plant with silvery variegated leaves.

Useful half-basket: 1. Parsley, planted as seedlings through the wire mesh. **2.** Tomato 'Tiny Tim'—place only one plant in a small basket, and allow it to tumble over the edge. **3.** The pink-mauve flowers of chives are an added attraction at the edge of the basket. **4.** Sweet basil.

Hot, sunny conditions: 1. Mesembryanthemums; daisy-like plants with succulent leaves, and flowers in electric colours, they only open in bright sunshine. **2.** *Helichrysum microphyllum* has tiny, grey leaves. **3.** *Gazania*, another daisy-like flower, is orange with black streaks and also closes in the evening. **4.** *Pyrethrum ptarmigaeflorum* has finely cut silver foliage.

Note: Although these plants happily tolerate hot, dry conditions, they are usually bought from a nursery where they will have been grown quickly and watered heavily. Keep them moist until they are established, then gradually reduce the water until this is given only when absolutely necessary.

AUTUMN WINTER

In autumn, clear baskets of all summer plants, and then check whether the compost – probably a solid mass of roots – needs replenishing. Retain moss, if possible, particularly if it has been kept moist through summer.

Rebuild the baskets, splitting ivy or periwinkles to give root clusters small enough to pass between the wire strands. For colour, plant peppers or heathers at the top. Ordinary winter heathers, often available in autumn, can later be transferred to the garden. Plant bulbs underneath them, or replace winter plants with polyanthus or pots of forced bulbs in early spring.

In permanently planted baskets, which rely on contrasts of foliage and form, include alpine plants and other small shrubs that will remain neat and tidy while developing their shapes.

Established greenery: 1. Variegated ivy. **2.** Trim back the summer growth on the bellflowers in autumn for a compact effect; remove all old leaves in winter. **3.** The small decorative peppers of *Capsicum frutescens* remain on the plant until mid-winter. **4.** The winter-flowering heather, *Erica carnea* 'Winter Beauty', has small, pink flowers from mid-winter onwards. Select good plants that will provide a foliage background.

Dry bulbs of short tulips or narcissi are planted for spring.

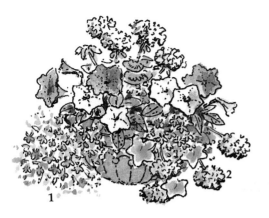

Terracotta pot: 1. Pale blue, trailing lobelia. **2.** Ivy-leaved geraniums, *Pelargonium peltatum* 'L'Elégante', have silver and green leaves and pale lavender flowers. **3.** White and blue petunias. **4.** Single, white geraniums (zonal pelargoniums).

Seasonal/sun: 1. Ivy-leaved geraniums, *Pelargonium peltatum*, are generally available in pinks or mauves. Choose a single variety, or mixture of colours, to set the overall colour scheme. **2.** Petunias tone in or contrast with the geraniums. Since they are available as small plants they can be forced into the side of the basket. **3.** Upright and trailing forms of bedding lobelia, in pale or dark blue, fill in rapidly between the other plants and create a blue haze. **4.** Choose upright geraniums (zonal pelargoniums) in colours that harmonize or contrast with the other flowers. **5.** *Helichrysum petiolatum* has grey, trailing foliage.

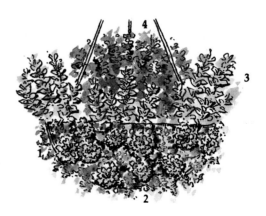

Winter only: 1. Various varieties of ivy, *Hedera*, create a tapestry effect over the sides of the basket. **2.** Ornamental pepper plants, *Capsicum frutescens*. **3.** Dark purple, half-hardy Cape heather, *Erica gracilis*.

Note: The pepper plants and heather will probably last only until mid-winter, although the latter will retain its form without flowers. Strip the box completely in early spring and replenish with forced plants such as polyanthus, *Primula polyantha*; and hyacinths.

Foliage/sun: 1. The houseleek, *Sempervivum*, has a striking foliage pattern. The separate plants gradually encroach to make a solid cover. **2.** Stonecrop, *Sedum acre*, has pale green, tiny, succulent foliage, and yellow flowers. **3.** Cushion spurge, *Euphorbia polychroma*, has lime-green to gold bracts in early summer. **4.** The coppery-purple foliage of the barberry, *Berberis thunbergii* 'Atropurpurea Nana', contrasts strongly with the cushion spurge and stone-crop. Select small plants to begin with. The barberry is deciduous.

WINDOW BOXES

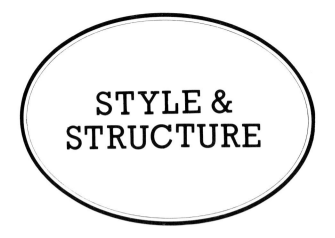

STYLE & STRUCTURE

It must be sturdy, durable and as large as possible without being out of proportion to its surroundings – plants need plenty of room to grow. Plain, rectangular shapes are often the most effective and easiest to handle. A simple box can be painted to match or contrast with the colour of the house. Alternatively, find one with a pattern that matches some architectural feature.

Planting styles are a matter of personal preference and should reflect the style of the house itself. They range from an informal mass of contrasting foliage, softened in front

Window boxes provide a wealth of colour and greenery and, if plants are selected with care, will remain charming all year.

However, practical considerations must come first. Stability and security are crucial, so it may be necessary to find or make special supporting brackets. Moisture, spilled compost and fallen leaves can all rot wooden window sills and frames, so make sure the box is surrounded by a layer of air. (Stand it on wooden blocks to lift it clear of the sill.)

Make sure, too, that the box can be reached easily and has free drainage – it will have to be regularly serviced and watered.

'Victorian Gothic' sash window.

Left: A luxuriant blend of trailing plants.

Traditional cottage window.

Bay window with an attractive iron railing.

with ivy, to formal arrangements of conifers and seasonal bedding plants. Whatever your choice, be sure to start with a sturdy box, sound, healthy plants, and appropriate compost.

Sun

19th-century window with pillared surround.

Modern window opening only at the top.

Shade

GREEN SKELETON

Sun

1. *Senecio greyi* forms the centrepiece; soft grey leaves provide year-round interest and it bears yellow flowers in summer. Choose a short, bushy plant and prune it occasionally to encourage lower growth and avoid legginess. **2.** The purple leaves of *Hebe* 'Midsummer Beauty' contrast with the grey foliage of the *Senecio*; flowers, borne in mid-summer, are blue. **3.** *Helichrysum petiolatum*; their abundant, grey-leafed, trailing stems make them ideal plants for this sunny position. They are only hardy during mild winters, and even then the box must be kept dry during the coldest weather. **4.** Spaces for seasonal plantings.

Shade

1. *Skimmia* 'Rubella' retains its dark green leaves throughout the year, and produces sprays of crimson buds in late autumn which open to form white flowers in spring. **2.** The bright, variegated foliage of the spotted laurels, *Aucuba crotonifolia*, provides a contrast in leaf shape and colour. They must be pruned occasionally to maintain the box's balanced shape. Both the *Skimmia* and the spotted laurels are normally available as established plants and will therefore be strong enough not to be overwhelmed by seasonal plants during the first summer. **3.** The ivy, *Hedera helix* 'Green Ripple', has attractive, long-lobed leaves. **4.** Spaces for seasonal plantings.

SPRING

There are two ways of providing colour during the spring – a period that, for the enthusiast, lasts from the flowering of the first narcissi and crocuses to the time when summer bedding plants are set out.

One way is to plant instant displays of forced bulbs, followed by polyanthus, cinerarias, calceolarias and even colourful hydrangeas – all of which are available from nurseries soon after mid-winter. Remember, though, that most of these will have been grown with some heating, and may suffer in a sudden cold spell.

The second way is to plant dry bulbs during the previous autumn: early-flowering narcissi 'February Gold' can be followed by cinerarias. Mid-season or late bulbs include the narcissus 'Geranium'. Wallflowers and forget-me-nots can also be planted to provide colour at the tail end of the season.

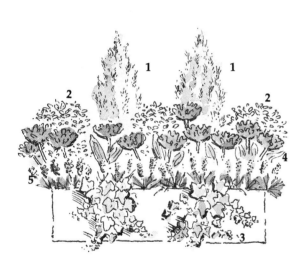

Traditional/sun: 1. The dwarf cypresses, *Chamaecyparis lawsoniana* 'Ellwoodii', are classic traditional conifers for window boxes, with a neat pyramidal habit and slow growth. They tend to 'brown' where other plants touch them and need regular watering during summer. **2.** *Hebe albicans* makes neat, grey-leaved, rounded bushes. Trim established plants to shape. **3.** The ivy, *Hedera helix* 'Glacier', has small, grey-green leaves. **4.** Seasonal planting of the short, double, early, scarlet tulip 'Carlton'. **5.** A line of grape hyacinths, *Muscari armeniacum* or *M. botryoides*, along the front edge of the box.

Formal/shade: 1. A pyramidal box, *Buxus sempervirens.* **2.** Spotted laurels, *Aucuba crotonifolia.* In the long term, the degree of variegation depends on the density of the shade – the deeper the shade, the slighter the variegation **3.** *Hebe* 'Subalpina' has distinctive, tiny, bright green leaves. **4.** The variegated ivy, *Hedera canariensis* 'Gloire de Marengo', tumbles down the side of the box. **5.** Seasonal planting of single-colour polyanthus, *Primula polyantha*, along the front edge of the box. **6.** Short narcissi, the early flowering 'February Gold', among the shrubs.

Informal/sun: 1. Lavender. *Lavandula* 'Hidcote' or *L.* 'Munstead' make compact plants. **2.** *Hebe* x *franciscana* 'Variegata' has a bright, variegated leaf. **3.** The sun rose, *Cistus* x *corbariensis.* Prune in early to mid-spring. **4.** The variegated ivy, *Hedera helix* 'Herald', with cream and white variegations. Trim before the new foliage appears. **5.** Short narcissi 'Fortune' have cream flowers and orange eyes.

Asymmetrical/sun: 1. *Elaeagnus pungens* 'Maculata' has bold variegated foliage. **2.** The dwarf broom, *Genista lydia*, produces an arching spray of yellow flowers in late spring. **3.** *Lonicera nitida* 'Baggesen's Gold' has tiny golden leaves. **4.** *Hebe* 'Autumn Glory', with green foliage. **5.** A seasonal planting of tulips, of the same type but in mixed colours, provides co-ordination but retains an informal effect. **6.** The small-leaved ivy, *Hedera helix* 'Goldheart', has a neat form and yellow centres to its leaves.

Informal/shade: 1. The strong, leathery leaves of *Viburnum davidii* create a distinctive foliage pattern. Prune the plants selectively in early spring to encourage new foliage from the base. **2.** Cineraria, *C. multiflora*, are available from florists and nurserymen from mid-spring. Choose three plants of the same colour—pale pink, for example—to co-ordinate the planting. **3.** The large, strongly veined leaves of the ivy, *Hedera canariensis*, complement those of the viburnum. Trim before new growth appears. **4.** Plantings of narcissus 'Silver Chimes'. **5.** Grape hyacinths, *Muscari*, form a thick band along the front of the box.

Seasonal/sun: 1. The grey foliage of *Helichrysum petiolatum* provides a year-round foreground in mild districts. **2.** Alternate clumps of crocuses and grape hyacinths, *Muscari*. **3.** Pale and dark blue hyacinths. **4.** Short, early narcissi 'Irene Copeland' are mixed with mid-season narcissi 'Fortune' to give a long flowering period.

Seasonal/shade: 1. Front edge of ivy, *Hedera helix* 'Chicago', provides a year-round green foil for colour. **2.** Alternate groups of yellow and white crocuses. Choose varieties that are pale in colour, with short stems; pale colours show better than bright ones in shade, and plants in shade often tend to go leggy. **3.** Planting of deep blue hyacinths 'Ostara' **4.** Pale, orange-eyed narcissi 'Geranium'; their later flowering adds to the continuity of colour.

Scented: 1. Lily of the valley, *Convallaria majalis*, flowers in late spring; its foliage remains attractive through summer. **2.** Pale yellow hyacinths 'City of Haarlem'. **3.** Christmas box, *Sarcococca*, has small, fragrant flowers during winter. **4.** Scented, jonquil-type narcissi 'Sugar Bush'. **5.** *Daphne odora* has fragrant flowers in winter as well as early spring. **6.** Jasmine, *Jasminum polyanthum*, is rather tender but may well survive in a protected box; it bears sweetly scented flowers in late spring. Cut back after flowering to encourage a bushy form.

SUMMER

The success of summer displays depends on the care with which boxes are prepared. Start by lifting bulbs and removing spent spring plants. Then dig the box through, incorporating a good, general fertilizer. Allow a generous handful to a 3ft (about 1m) wide box. If you are using new compost, or if the box was unused during winter and spring, soak it well and leave it for a day before planting.

Be sure to water bought plants thoroughly before planting out – a dry plant set into dry soil is a recipe for disaster, no matter how much water is applied afterwards.

Window boxes must be kept moist. The amount of water, and frequency of watering, will depend on the boxes' aspect and the weather. Plants are unhappy when they are standing in puddles – nor do they like to remain dry for long periods. A liquid or foliar feed is recommended at regular intervals.

Finally, remove faded flower heads: by directing the plant's energy away from seed-making, this will encourage more flowers.

Asymmetrical/sun: 1. *Elaeagnus.* **2.** Broom. **3.** *Lonicera.* **4.** *Hebe* has purple flowers in late summer. **5.** Pale lemon French marigolds, *Tagetes patula*, are mixed with: **6.** Marguerites, *Chrysanthemum frutescens.* **7.** Alyssum has small bunches of white flowers and is grouped along the front of the box.

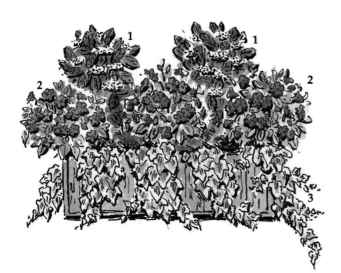

Informal/shade: 1. Viburnum. **2.** Replace the cineraria with red busy Lizzie, *Impatiens sultanii* . The plants will eventually merge into the viburnum and cascade over the front and sides of the box, producing a tiered effect. **3.** Ivy.

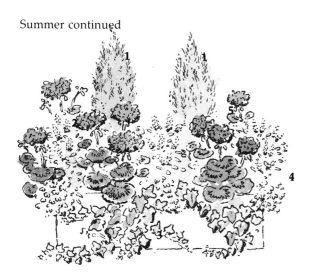

Traditional/sun: 1. Dwarf cypresses. **2.** *Hebe* has white flowers in late summer. **3.** Ivy, with new growth of soft greeny-grey. **4.** Upright blue lobelia. **5.** A scarlet geranium, *Pelargonium* 'Paul Crampel' (zonal).

Formal/shade: 1. Trim the box to maintain shape when new growth appears. **2.** Cut back the spotted laurel whenever necessary to keep its proportion and discourage loss of lower foliage. **3.** *Hebe* has small, white flowers in late summer. **4.** Cut back the larger trails of variegated ivy to encourage busy growth at its base. **5.** A line of crimson and white, fibrous-rooted begonias, *B. semperflorens*. **6.** Half-hardy fuchsias with white and crimson bells, 'Snowcap' perhaps.

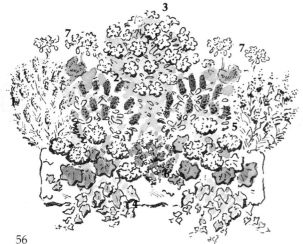

Informal/sun: 1. The lavender produces flower spikes in mid-summer. **2.** *Hebe* has pale mauve flowers in late summer which continue into autumn. **3.** The bronze buds of the sun rose open to form pure white flowers. **4.** The ivy is at its best in early summer when fresh leaves cover the plant. **5.** The pale pink flowers of the ivy-leaved geranium, *Pelargonium peltatum* 'Galilee', tumble down the front of the box. **6.** Trailing lobelia. **7.** Single, white-flowered geraniums (zonal pelargoniums).

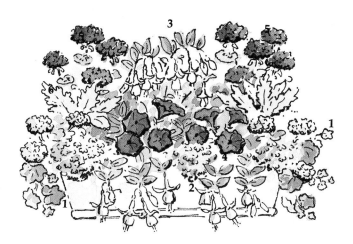

Seasonal/sun: 1. Ivy-leaved geraniums, *Pelargonium peltatum* L'Elégante', have variegated leaves and very pale blush flowers. **2.** Trailing fuchsias of the same colour as: **3.** An upright half-hardy fuchsia. **4.** Dark purple petunias. **5.** Deep cerise geraniums, *Pelargonium* 'William Tell' (zonal). **6.** Cineraria, *C. maritima*, has silver foliage **7.** Pale blue, trailing lobelia.

Seasonal/shade: 1. Variegated form of Virginia creeper, *Ampelopsis brevipedunculata* 'Elegans', has cream- and pink-tinged leaves; the pink picks up the flowers of: **2.** Fuchsias. **3.** Choose flame nettles, *Coleus*, that will harmonize with the pink and pale-green colour scheme. They are occasionally available in a clear lime green, which would be ideal. **4.** Pale pink busy Lizzie, *Impatiens sultanii*, picks up the pink in the fuchsias.

Foliage/shade: 1. Creeping Jenny, *Lysimachia nummularia*, has tumbling trails of bright green foliage with yellow flowers. **2.** Hart's tongue fern, *Phyllitis scolopendrium*; other hardy ferns could be used. **3.** Mexican mock orange, *Choisya ternata*, has bright green foliage and white flowers; it must be pruned lightly at regular intervals to keep its size in balance with the rest of the box. **4.** Solomon's seal, *Polygonatum* x *hybridum*, has arching straps of grey-green foliage carrying simple, tubular, white flowers.

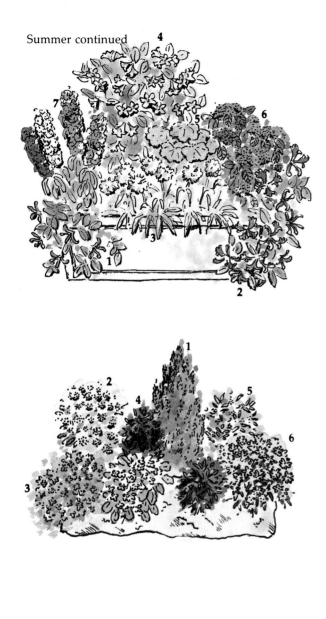

Summer continued

Scented: 1. The honeysuckle, *Lonicera periclymenum* 'Belgica', flowers in early summer. **2.** *L. periclymenum* 'Serotina' is in bloom from mid-,to late summer. **3.** Pinks, *Dianthus* 'Mrs. Sinkins', with white, scented flowers and grey-green foliage. **4.** *Abelia chinensis* has fragrant, pink-tinted white flowers. **5.** Scented-leaf geranium, *Pelargonium tomentosum*; its leaves are peppermint scented. **6.** The common name, cherry pie, suggests the scent of *Heliotropium*; it has flat umbels of blue-purple flowers. **7.** Stocks, *Matthiola incana* of the Ten Week variety, tucked in wherever possible.

Alpine: 1. Dark green, dwarf juniper, *Juniperus communis* 'Compressa'. **2.** Perennial alyssum, *A. saxatile*, has silver, grey-green leaves; it bears yellow flowers in late spring. **3.** Aubretia, *A. deltoidea*, bears purple and blue flowers in early summer. Trim back well after flowering to retain its bushy shape and encourage a second crop of flowers. **4.** *Lithospermum diffusum* 'Grace Ward' has bright blue flowers later in summer, and upright, evergreen leaves. **5.** The lemon-scented thyme, *T.* x *citriodorus*, has variegated, scented leaves. **6.** The phlox, *P. subulata*, is a tumbling mat of tiny, dark green leaves covered with pale pink flowers in late spring. Trim after flowering to retain shape. **7.** *Arabis albida* has evergreen foliage and white flowers from late winter to early summer.

All these plants require a neutral, or slightly acid, free-draining compost.

Roses: 1. Miniature roses; plant at about 10in (25cm) intervals. Their colours are complemented by: **2.** Carpet of bedding plants.

Suggested combinations are: **1.** Pale pink 'Dresden Doll' and **2.** Pale blue lobelia; **1.** Creamy yellow 'Yellow Doll' and **2.** Pure white alyssum, *A. maritimum* 'Little Dorrit' syn. 'Little Gem'; **1.** White-flowered 'Pour Toi' and **2.** One of the many varieties of French marigold, *Tagetes patula*, with orange-yellow flowers. The last-mentioned combination is shown in the illustration.

All bedding plants must be newly planted each season; it is important to feed the roses and for them to have as much space as possible.

Herbs: 1. A small bay, *Laurus nobilis*, in the centre of the box. **2.** Sweet basil, *Ocimum basilicum*, is not hardy, and is normally bought as a growing plant in the spring of each year. **3.** Rosemary, *Rosmarinus officinalis*. **4.** Common thyme, *Thymus vulgaris*. **5.** Parsley, *Petroselinum crispum*, is planted along the front edge with: **6.** Chives, *Allium schoenoprasum*. **7.** Mint, *Mentha*, is separated off at the end of the box by a vertical division to restrain invasive roots.

Note: Herb boxes should be in an open position that catches the sun for at least half the day.

Useful: 1. Alpine strawberries, *Fragaria vesca*; the small, sweet fruits tumble over the edge of the box. **2.** Tomatoes; 'Tiny Tim' is a tumbling variety with small fruit. **3.** Standard size tomatoes; allow them to run up to four trusses (bunches) of fruit and then stop. **4.** Tarragon, *Artemisia dracunculus*, is a useful herb for summer salads and poultry. **5.** Plant parsley, *Petroselinum crispum*, in all the gaps.

Note: To support the crop, the compost must be well fed with organic material and the box must be watered copiously throughout summer.

Low maintenance/shade: 1. Periwinkles, *Vinca minor*, have dark green foliage with mid-blue, star-like flowers. **2.** *Euonymus radicans* 'Variegatus' has small, variegated leaves and a neat, trailing habit. **3.** Plantain lilies, *Hosta fortunei* 'Albo-marginata', have a strong pattern of foliage with white margins on the green leaves. **4.** x *Osmarea burkwoodii* is a compact shrub with dark green leaves and fragrant, white flowers.

AUTUMN WINTER

Although most summer plants come to an end early in autumn, there are some exceptions. Small-flowered begonias are at their best, busy Lizzie is effective if overgrown, and geraniums continue to flower, though in less profusion than in summer. However, these are only general rules – one early frost can reduce a box of busy Lizzie to rubbery stalks in the course of a night.

Bulbs and wallflowers are best planted by mid-autumn, and all summer plants should therefore be removed before this date. Dig through the box thoroughly and apply bone-meal to the soil to encourage root development. If the box has become dry, soak it and let it drain well before planting.

Plant bulbs evenly and at the correct depth – all but the smallest specimens should be set as far down into the box as possible.

Prune and shape permanent plants to keep the box tidy during winter.

Traditional/sun: 1. Dwarf cypresses. **2.** *Hebe*; trim the bushes lightly after flowering, and remove the dead flowers. **3.** Trim the ivy before new growth begins in spring. **4.** Plant a solid line of *Scilla sibirica* or *Chionodoxa* to make a blue edge in spring. **5.** Plant the pale pink hyacinth 'Pink Pearl'—or choose a colour and variety you prefer—to combine with *Scilla*.

Formal/shade: 1. Box. **2.** Spotted laurel. **3.** Trim the *Hebe* lightly to remove dead flowers. **4.** Variegated ivy. **5.** Plant groups of white crocuses, 'Jeanne d'Arc', for spring flowering. **6.** The half-hardy Cape heather, *Erica gracilis*, provides colour until mid-winter.

Plant white, short-stemmed narcissi 'Horn of Plenty' around and below the heather.

Bulbs will flower in a shady box provided they are bought new each year. Always be sure to select short varieties; the plants will invariably be elongated by the relative absence of light.

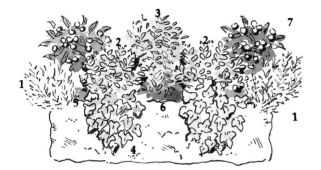

Informal/sun/autumn and winter: 1. Lavender. Trim off flower spikes as they fade and cut the bushes back to neat shapes. **2.** The *Hebe* flowers well into early winter, given favourable weather. **3.** Prune the sun rose lightly whenever necessary but leave heavy pruning until spring. **4.** Leave the ivy in during winter to soften the face of the box when seasonal plants are removed. **5, 6.** Fill spaces left when the summer planting is removed by edging the front of the box with grape hyacinths, *Muscari*, or short, early tulips, *Tulipa kaufmanniana*. Before planting the bulbs, work in bone-meal and thoroughly prepare the soil to prevent uneven flowering. **7.** Plant narcissi 'Irene Copeland' under winter cherries, *Solanum capsicastrum* to give creamy white and apricot flowers in spring.

Foliage/sun: 1. Honeysuckle, *Lonicera japonica* 'Auto-reticulata', with a compact growth of golden-veined leaves. Keep the plants clipped back to encourage this. **2.** *Hebe pinguifolia* 'Pagei' makes a low, spreading mat of grey-green leaves. **3.** *Sedum spectabile* also has grey-green leaves, with pink flowers in autumn; the plants die back in winter. **4.** Rue, *Ruta graveolens*, with finely divided blue-green leaves. **5.** *Euonymus japonicus* 'Aureovariegatus' is a compact, laurel-like shrub with creamy yellow, young leaves.

Informal/shade: 1. Viburnum. **2.** A line of polyanthus, *Primula polyantha*, retains its green foliage during winter. Any short-growing, established plants that are available in autumn – pansies, *Viola* x *wittrockiana* or primulas, *P.* 'Wanda', for example — can be used provided they tolerate shade sufficiently to flower in spring. **3.** Short, early, clear yellow narcissi 'February Gold'. When they have flowered, use polyanthus, already forced into bloom, to fill the box and provide a display through to late spring **4.** Ivy.

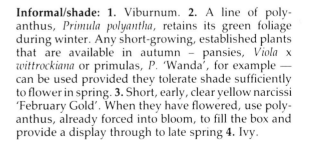

Overleaf: A classic window box overflowing with geraniums. The coral pink of the blooms is beautifully offset by the stone walls and the dull green window frames and balcony wall.

FRONT GARDENS

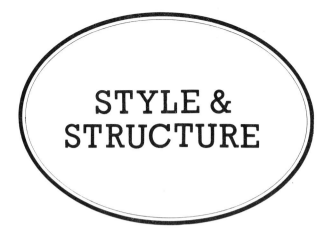

STYLE & STRUCTURE

Terraced houses. A central display will create a focal point in the garden area.

Front gardens are infinitely variable. Some guard their owner's privacy; others, more exuberant, add a personal touch to otherwise staid and uninteresting streets. Some very impressive gardens add nothing to a neighbourhood; others may be overgrown and untrained but nevertheless break a harsh line of walls to fresh and charming effect.

Traffic pollution can be a serious problem if you live on or near a main road. In these circumstances avoid glaucous plants whose leaves will become clogged with dirt. Rely instead on tough evergreens that can be washed down. The foliage of deciduous shrubs and herbaceous plants changes each year, and doesn't suffer so badly from dust and dirt.

Allow for a generous footpath leading from the road to your front door, and make sure there are easy links to side or garage entrances. Plants can be used to soften their edges without affecting access. Extend the hard surface, even if only in the form of stepping stones, to allow for easy window cleaning.

Climbing plants add visually to the appearance of your house, as well as giving pleasure to passers-by. Choose the variety carefully, and remember that caring for climbing roses can be time-consuming,

Double-fronted house. Set off its classic lines with formal trees and shrubs.

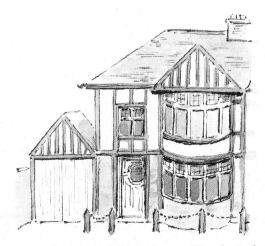

Semi-detached, half-timbered house. Use plants that echo architectural features.

Left: Paving stones provide a perfect foil for flowers, while climbers follow the lines of the doorway and rounded front.

whereas self-clinging Virginia creeper only needs annual pruning to restrict its growth.

Boundaries to front gardens range from hedges to picket fences and brick walls. If you have a choice of treatment, take into account the amount of privacy you want, whether the area needs to be protected from the wind, and whether an open garden would encourage vandalism.

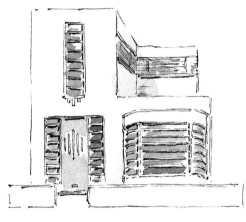

Bold, geometrical 1930s style. Plants should have bold, interesting shapes.

Traditional cottage. Grow a profusion of plants, but keep them well trimmed.

GREEN SKELETON

Sun

1. *Teucrium fruticans* has pale green leaves with white undersides, and blue flowers in summer. **2.** *Hebe pinguifolia* 'Pagei' forms a low mat of grey foliage. **3.** *Ozothamnus rosmarinifolium* forms spires of grey-green foliage similar to rosemary. **4.** *Juniperus squamata* 'Meyeri' is a semi-erect, grey-green conifer. **5.** *Helxine soleirolii* spreads its carpet in the shade of the low wall. **6.** *Yucca filamentosa* bears spikes of cream flowers in mid-summer after two or three years' growth. **7.** *Senecio greyi* can be adapted to any shape. It has yellow flowers in summer. **8.** *Convolvulus cneorum* produces white flowers in summer and has year-round, bright silver foliage. **9.** Spaces for seasonal plantings of your choice.

Shade

1. *Osmanthus heterophyllus* 'Variegatus' has compact, variegated, holly-like foliage. **2.** *Skimmia* 'Rubella', an easy evergreen, bears pink-tinged buds in winter. **3.** The low mat of foliage produced by *Cotoneaster dammeri* softens the lines of the paving. White flowers in early summer are followed later by red berries. **4.** Variegated holly, *Ilex aquifolium* 'Silver Queen'; it must be lightly pruned to retain its shape and control its size. **5.** Plantain lilies, *Hosta glauca*, provide a strong foliage base for the holly during spring and summer. **6.** *Helxine soleirolii* thrives in shade and produces an unequalled effect of cushioned abundance. **7.** The ornamental cherry laurel, *Prunus laurocerasus* 'Schip-kaensis', is of spreading habit with narrow leaves. It carries white flowers in late spring.

8. The hydrangea, *H. villosa*, softens the corner; its pale mauve flower clusters appear in late summer. **9.** The ivy, *Hedera* 'Cristata', has distinctive, round leaves with curled edges. **10.** Spaces for seasonal plantings.

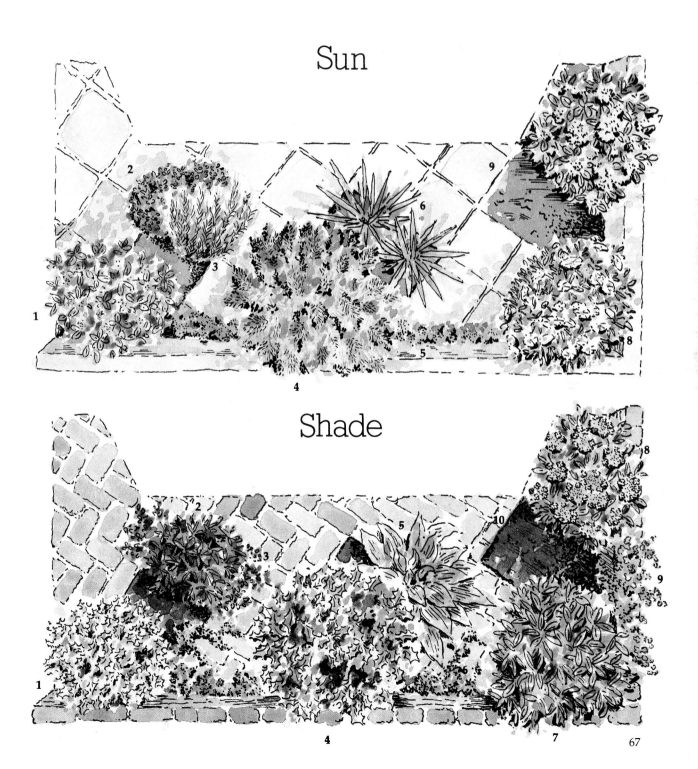

Sun

Shade

SPRING

The first indications of spring are more immediately noticeable in front gardens than in almost any other area. Take advantage of this by including early flowering shrubs like yellow winter jasmine, sweet-scented *Mahonia japonica*, which also has yellow flowers, or green-stemmed *Kerria japonica*.

Bulbs are another priority. The appearance of narcissi, tulips and daffodils is a sure indication that winter is over, and a representative selection in a small front garden has a dash and impact that would be lost in a larger area. Regularly remove faded blooms to maintain the display, and lift the bulbs as their foliage yellows. Plant fresh ones every year and infiltrate spent bulbs in an unimportant corner.

Fresh foliage is equally important. Plant some deciduous shrubs including climbers like a glory vine or Virginia creeper.

In very protected gardens new growth will immediately attract aphids, particularly if plants are against a warm wall. Spray immediately; they distort soft shoots.

Shade: 1. Lime tree, *Tilia* x *europaea*. **2.** A pair of mop-headed bay trees, *Laurus nobilis*, in tubs. Trim to shape in late spring before new foliage begins, or pinch back new foliage. **3.** A second pair of bays to complement **2.** Treat as **2. 4.** *Mahonia aquifolium* has good, year-round foliage and can partially withstand drips caused by aphids feeding on the limes. **5.** The hydrangeas, *H. hortensia* are dormant. Remove old flower heads as the new buds swell and the danger of heavy frost passes. **6.** Formality is preserved by the lines of the Japanese quinces, *Chaenomeles speciosa* 'Pink Lady', which flower against the white stucco house, starting in early spring. **7.** A trellis column and, **12,** a large vase counterbalance the tree. The column carries *Schizophragma hydrangeoides*, now dormant, and the vase is full of narcissi 'Irene Copeland' in pale colours. **8.** *Clematis montana* 'Rubens' flowers pink at the tail end of spring. **9.** *Skimmia* 'Rubella' and *S. japonica* continue the rather formal, evergreen perimeter planting. *S.* 'Rubella' produces white flowers following pink-tinged buds. **10.** The ivy, *Hedera canariensis* 'Gloire de Marengo', carries its variegated foliage throughout the year. **11.** Plantain lilies, *Hosta glauca*, are dormant. **13.** Hardy fuchsias have been cut back by winter frost.

Sun and shade: 1. Early flowers begin to break from the branched framework of wisteria, *Wistaria sinensis*. **2.** Winter jasmine, *Jasminum nudiflorum*, produces an early display of bright yellow flowers on leafless stems. **3.** The climbing rose 'Handel' is a bare framework. **4.** Seasonal plants include early tulips, crocuses, and narcissi. **5.** *Daphne odora* has perfumed, white flowers in late winter and early spring. **6.** The Japanese quince, *Chaenomeles speciosa* 'Nivalis', produces white flowers before leaves appear. It is also available in reds and pinks, so choose a variety appropriate to the colour of the brickwork. **7.** *Ceanothus* x 'Autumnal Blue' is an evergreen shrub that can be trained against the wall. **8.** *Senecio greyi* keeps its silver foliage throughout the year. **9.** Central vase filled with double, late tulips 'Mount Tacoma'. **10.** An edging of lavender, *Lavandula* 'Munstead'. **11.** The camellia, *C. japonica* 'Gloire de Nantes', has large, rose-pink flowers and glossy, evergreen leaves. **12.** Lady's mantle, *Alchemilla mollis*, is dormant. **13.** The hellebore, *Helleborus corsicus*, has pale green and cream flowers throughout early spring.

SPECIAL

Dense shade: 1. Lime or cherry trees. **2.** A decorative fence that can be washed free of drips from the trees. **3.** Narcissus bulbs planted under gravel for early spring flowering while the trees are bare. **4.** Periwinkles, *Vinca major*, with good, green foliage and single, blue flowers in early summer provide a tough evergreen edging. **5.** Vases contain seasonal plantings which can be changed when they are affected by the deep shade. Possibilities include: tulips, forced hydrangeas or primulas in spring; half-hardy fuchsias in summer; chrysanthemums in autumn; and Cape heather, *Erica gracilis*, or winter cherries, *Solanum capsicastrum*, in winter.

SPECIAL

Spring continued

◁ **Sun: 1.** Climbing roses, the classic 'Albertine' and 'New Dawn', arch over the doorway. **2.** Green holly, *Ilex* 'J.C. Van Tol'. **3.** The flowers of *Viburnum tinus* 'Eve Price' last into early spring. Prune after flowering. **4.** Lavender, *Lavandula* 'Hidcote'. **5.** A selection of honeysuckles: *Lonicera repens*, *L.* 'Belgica', and *L.* 'Serotina'. **6.** The Mexican mock orange, *Choisya ternata*, has good evergreen foliage. **7.** The hydrangea, *H. petiolaris*, is dormant on the wall. **8.** *Cotoneaster horizontalis* grows along the base of the wall. **9.** The southernwood, *Artemisia abrotanum*, is semi-dormant after winter. **10.** London pride, *Saxifraga umbrosa*. **11.** Tulips and narcissi. Leave them to naturalize in seasonal planting areas. **12.** Perennials; *Doronicum* has yellow flower heads in early spring. **13.** *Forsythia suspensa* produces yellow flowers against the wall. **14.** Rosemary, *Rosmarinus officinalis*, flowers in early spring. Prune the forsythia and rosemary after flowering.

◁ **Permanent/sun: 1.** *Abutilon megapotamicum* produces bright red and yellow flowers through summer to autumn. **2.** Shrubby veronicas, *Hebe pinguifolia*, have blue-grey leaves and tiny, white flowers in early summer. **3.** *Senecio monroi* has year-round, attractive, grey foliage. **4.** *Iris stylosa*, the first of the perennial irises, produces blue flowers in late winter. **5.** *Hypericum elatum* 'Elstead' has yellow flowers in summer and brilliant salmon red fruits in autumn. **6.** *Potentilla* 'Primrose Beauty' has creamy yellow flowers throughout summer. **7.** *Geranium sanguineum* bears dainty, cerise flowers in summer and is of compact habit. **8.** A sun rose, *Cistus pulverulentus*, with good, year-round foliage and cerise flowers in summer. **9.** *Achillea ptarmica* 'Perry's White' has flat-topped clusters of white flowers in summer. **10.** Group of small gum trees, *Eucalyptus gunnii*. Cut back some plants to produce new silver foliage and allow others to grow up and display their equally interesting, year-round foliage; the group will be visible from inside the house. **11.** *Geranium* 'Johnson's Blue' produces an abundance of single, blue flowers in late spring and early summer. **12.** The broom, *Cytisus x praecox* 'All Gold', flowers yellow in early summer. **13.** *Olearia x scilloniensis* has grey leaves and white flowers in early summer. **14.** *Cotoneaster congestus* is low growing and makes good cover. **15.** The rock rose, *Helianthemum* 'Ben More', produces orange flowers throughout summer.

Paved/sun/summer: 1. The potato vine, *Solanum crispum*, produces pale blue flowers throughout summer. **2.** The myrtle, *Myrtus communis*, has neat, aromatic, evergreen foliage, and tiny, white flowers. **3.** Cranesbill, *Geranium ibericum*, has bright blue flowers. **4.** The broom, *Genista lydia*, grows in graceful strands of yellow-covered branches which overhang the edge of the pot. **5.** Seasonal plantings of geraniums, *Pelargonium* 'Orange Fizz' (zonal); marguerites *Felicia amelloides*; and *Helichrysum petiolatum*. **6.** The hardy Chinese fan palm, *Trachycarpus fortunei*, gives a faintly tropical feel to the garden. **7.** *Pittosporum tenuifolium* 'Garnettii' has variegated foliage with a tinge of pink. **8.** *Santolina chamaecyparissus* forms a mound of grey foliage with yellow, dome-shaped flowers in early summer. **9.** *Cordyline indivisa* creates a dramatic, architectural form. **10.** Lemon and orange French marigolds, *Tagetes patula*, are edged with pale blue lobelia. (See page 85 for this garden in winter.)

SUMMER

Summer is the time to indulge yourself in a spectacular display of seasonal flowers and soft foliage.

Colour schemes can be co-ordinated or contrasted with exterior paintwork. Scarlet geraniums match a scarlet front door, or stand out sharply against black and white. The soft pinks and blues of petunias blend beautifully with grey-green paintwork or aged wood. Bricks are an effective foil for white and pale pink busy Lizzie. If house walls are a neutral shade you will be able to experiment, changing your choice of plants – and colours – from one year to the next.

Regular weeding and spraying against greenfly is important in summer. Removing spent flower heads is another priority. If the dead flower remains the plant will put all its energy into producing seeds at the expense of new blooms. Ask your nurseryman how much of the stem to cut off when dead-heading – procedures vary with different plants.

Shade: 1. The lime is in full leaf. Wash the plants ▷ underneath it every day with a hose, to remove drips. **2.** Bay trees. Feed throughout early summer, if necessary. **3.** Bays. Treat as 2. **4.** *Mahonia* flowers on old wood in late spring. The density of shade during the previous summer will affect the ripening of the wood and hence the flowering. **5.** The hydrangeas are in full leaf. Apply colourant to the soil to produce blue flowers in neutral or alkaline soil. **6.** Tie in and prune the Japanese quinces after flowering. **7.** The *Schizophragma* has large, creamy white flower heads in midsummer. **8.** The clematis has abundant flowers in early summer. Prune after flowering to keep tidy. **9.** *Skimmia.* **10.** Ivy. **11.** The plantain lilies provide a stunning foliage display at the base of the clematis. Depending on light levels, there may be flower spikes in late summer. **12.** Vase filled with shade-loving annuals, such as half-hardy fuchsias and busy Lizzie, *Impatiens.* **13.** Hardy fuchsias show a new flush of growth.

Sun and shade: 1. The last flowers of the wisteria still show among the foliage. Reduce side growth by about three-quarters in late summer, to encourage flowering spurs. **2.** Carry out any trimming or pruning on the winter jasmine after flowering. **3.** The rose 'Handel' has cream flowers touched with rosy pink at the edges. Remove faded blooms to encourage further flowering. **4.** Seasonal planting; try busy Lizzie, *Impatiens,* in shady borders and among shrubs where it will fill in spaces naturally. In early summer, plant one or two groups of chrysanthemums to flower in autumn. **5.** *Daphne.* **6.** The Japanese quince is now in leaf; prune if necessary after flowering. **7.** *Ceanothus* starts flowering in late summer and continues until early autumn. **8.** Remove the yellow flowers of *Senecio* immediately after they fade, and prune the bush lightly to retain shape. **9.** The central vase has a major seasonal planting of geraniums (ivy-leaved, and zonal pelargoniums), edged with petunias and lobelia. Choose colours to complement the pink busy Lizzie. **10.** The lavender has short, blue flower spikes. **11.** After the camellia has flowered, feed and mulch it with peat mixed with bone-meal or well-rotted manure. **12.** Lady's mantle has attractive foliage with sprays of cream flowers. **13.** Hellebore.

SPECIAL

Vandal-proof: 1. A steel bar, with pyramid shapes, on the top of the wall discourages sitting. **2.** Vases planted with barberries, *Berberis candidula*, thorny dwarf shrubs of compact, rounded habit and with bright yellow flowers in late spring and early summer. **3.** *B. gagnepainii*. Its upright stems form a low dense hedge. **4.** *B. julianiae*, a strong and thorny, evergreen hedge with yellow flowers in late spring. **5.** Spanish gorse, *Genista hispanica*, forms an edge to the pathway. It has yellow flowers in early summer.

Summer continued

Sun: 1. Climbing roses; 'Albertine' blooms in one lovely flush of apricot pink flowers, and 'New Dawn' flowers recurrently in pale pink. **2.** Holly. **3.** Viburnum. **4.** The lavender has old-fashioned, strong purple flowers. **5.** The different varieties of honeysuckle give a spread of flowering times and colours. **6.** The Mexican mock orange produces white, star-like flowers in early summer. Prune, if necessary, immediately after flowering. **7.** The hydrangea has 'lacecap' flowers during late summer. **8.** The small, blush flowers of *Cotoneaster* attract bees. **9.** The southernwood has attractive, finely divided, greygreen foliage. **10.** London pride produces pale pink flower heads on long stems. **11.** Prepare small seed beds and sow patches of annuals including marigolds, *Calendula*; love-in-a-mist, *Nigella*; night-scented stocks, *Matthiola bicornis*; and biennials including hollyhocks, *Althaea rosea*; and sweet Williams, *Dianthus barbatus*. Introduce some chrysanthemums and dahlias for autumn colour. **12.** Traditional perennials include lupins, *Lupinus*; delphiniums; bergamot; *Eriogonum*; *Achillea*; Michaelmas daisies, *Aster novae-angliae*. **13.** Forsythia. **14.** Rosemary.

Low maintenance/sun: 1. The Kolomikta vine, *Actinidia kolomikta*, has pale pink and cream foliage. **2.** *Deutzia* x *kalmiiflora* has garlands of blush pink flowers in early summer. **3.** Dwarf lavender, *Lavandula* 'Munstead', has rich purple flowers. **4.** The sun rose, *Cistus* x *corbariensis*, has white flowers with maroon eyes. **5.** The glory vine, *Vitis coignetiae*, has handsome leaves throughout summer which turn to marvellous colours in autumn. **6.** The daisy bush, *Olearia* x *haastii* bears white, daisy-like flowers and good, grey-green foliage. **7.** The weeping pear, *Pyrus salicifolia*, has arching bands of silver-grey foliage and off-white flowers in early summer. **8.** *Hebe* 'Bowles Variety' contrasts bronze foliage with pale lavender flowers. **9.** The barberries, *Berberis verruculosa*, are compact and have small, dark green leaves with white undersides, and yellow flowers. **10.** Lawn or paving. **11.** Spanish gorse, *Genista hispanica*, grows in neat mounds covered with yellow flowers in late spring. **12.** The clematis, *C. armandii*, is evergreen with white flowers in spring. **13.** Stepping-stones to windows and drive. **14.** Tubs of seasonal plants: geraniums (zonal pelargoniums), petunias, etc.

Paved/shade/summer: 1. *Hydrangea petiolaris* is self clinging with 'lace-cap' flowers. **2.** The Irish yew, *Taxus* 'Fastigiata', forms an upright, dark green column. **3.** The ivy, *Hedera helix* 'Sagittaefolia', has a small, distinctive leaf shape. **4.** *Daphne odora*. **5.** Seasonal plantings in pink and purple: busy Lizzie, *Impatiens*; and half-hardy fuchsias. **6.** *Fatsia japonica* has bold, evergreen foliage. **7.** The slender stems of the bamboo, *Arundinaria nitida*, break the shape of the window. They can be thinned out if the room loses too much light. **8.** *Elaeagnus pungens* 'Aureo-variegata' has strong, cream-and-yellow-flushed foliage. **9.** *Kerria japonica* 'Variegata' carries green-and-white, variegated foliage on graceful, arching stems. **10.** A seasonal planting of bellflowers, *Campanula isophylla*, surrounds pale pink, fibrous-rooted begonias, *B. semperflorens*. (See page 79 for this garden in winter.)

AUTUMN

As summer and herbaceous plants die back and shrubs lose their leaves, the evergreen structure of your garden is revealed. Look at it critically; evergreens are the backbone of any garden and this is the time to decide on changes or improvements.

Late-flowering shrubs like hydrangeas, fuchsias and *Ceratostigma* continue to provide colour, possibly until winter-flowering plants start to bloom. Given a mild autumn or Indian summer, many half-hardy perennials like geraniums will also continue to flower well into the season. Brightly coloured foliage and berried shrubs add to the vivid display.

Wallflowers and other biennials must be put in their flowering positions, and autumn is also the time to plant bulbs like narcissi, hyacinths, daffodils and tulips for a spring display.

Finally, remember to tidy away fallen leaves and remove frost-damaged seasonal plants.

Shade: 1. The leaves of the lime turn yellow and fall. **2.** ▷ Bay trees. **3.** Bays. **4.** The *Mahonia* foliage hardens and turns dark green and purple. **5.** The hydrangeas, in full flower during late summer and early autumn, fade gracefully as the blooms age. **6.** Japanese quinces. **7.** *Schizophragma.* **8.** Clematis can sometimes have a second flush of flowering in late summer. **9.** *Skimmia*; *S. japonica* carries red berries. **10.** New summer growth on the ivy hardens. **11.** The leaves fade on the plantain lilies. **12.** Fuchsias and busy Lizzie continue until the first frost. **13.** The hardy fuchsias continue flowering through autumn into early winter.

Sun and shade: 1. The wisteria leaves turn golden-yellow as they fall. **2.** Winter jasmine. **3.** Tie long growths of the rose 'Handel' into the wall or other branches to form a framework for next year. Shorten flowering spurs and new side growth to encourage flowering wood. **4.** Busy Lizzie will survive until the first sharp frost. Chrysanthemums flower in late autumn. **5.** *Daphne.* **6.** Japanese quince. **7.** *Ceanothus.* Prune lightly when flowering finishes. **8.** *Senecio.* **9.** Geraniums and other seasonal plants continue until late autumn, depending on the weather. **10.** When flowering finishes, shear over the lavender to remove dead spikes and maintain its shape. **11.** Camellia. **12.** Remove dead flower heads from lady's mantle and generally tidy the plant. **13.** Hellebore.

SPECIAL

Flat conversion: 1. The entrance is widened allowing the border, **2,** to be extended. Rose of Sharon, *Hypericum calycinum*, makes a solid strip of foliage, with yellow flowers in summer. **3.** The rubbish enclosure built into the outside wall has an asphalted, recessed top filled with *Cotoneaster salicifolius* 'Repens'. **4.** Paved overspill area for cartons and plastic bags. **5.** The ornamental cherry, *Prunus subhirtella* 'Autumnalis Rosea', produces clouds of pale pink flowers during milder winter spells. **6.** Underplant the tree with Mexican mock orange, *Choisya ternata*; it bears white flowers in early summer. **7.** The seat is decorative—a sculptural element—and not necessarily for sitting on. **8.** Seasonal plantings in the pedestal vases on each side of the door create interesting colour contrasts. Depending on aspect, try cineraria or dwarf broom, *Genista lydia*, in spring; geraniums (zonal pelargoniums), petunias or *Helichrysum petiolatum* in summer; ornamental peppers, *Capsicum frutescens*, in autumn; and dry bulbs under winter cherries, *Solanum capsicastrum*, in winter.

The wall beside the path is covered with Virginia creeper, *Parthenocissus quinquefolia*.

SPECIAL

Autumn continued

◁ **Sun: 1.** Tie in the long shoots of the roses, reduce short growths and generally make the plants tidy. **2.** Holly. **3.** Viburnum. **4.** Shear over the lavender to remove dead spikes and generally shape the plants. **5.** Keep the honeysuckles under control by removing the longer shoots. **6.** Mexican mock orange. **7.** Leave the graceful, faded flowers on the hydrangea. **8.** Berries start to appear on the *Cotoneaster*. **9.** Make the southernwood into a compact bush for winter by shearing it over. **10.** London pride retains its foliage. **11.** Seasonal plants continue to flower until early autumn—dahlias until the first frost. **12.** Late-flowering perennials include Michaelmas daisies and *Eriogonum*. **13.** Forsythia. **14.** Rosemary.

◁ **Permanent/shade: 1.** Gold-centred, green leaves of ivy, *Hedera helix* 'Jubilee', form a neat, compact growth. **2.** Once established, *Pachysandra terminalis* makes a perfect ground cover with an interesting leaf pattern. **3.** The camellia, *C.* x *williamsii* 'J.C. Williams', has semi-single, clear-pink flowers during winter. **4.** The plantain lily, *Hosta fortunei* 'Albopicta', has cream and green leaves, and flowers in mid-summer. **5.** The arching stems of Solomon's seal, *Polygonatum* x *hybridum*, bear white flowers in early summer. **6.** *Osmanthus heterophyllus* has neat-growing, holly-like leaves. **7.** The regal fern, *Osmunda regalis*, with its distinguished foliage, makes a superb central plant. **8.** A ground cover mat of *Ajuga reptans*, has blue flower spikes at the beginning of summer. **9.** The year-round, leathery foliage of *Viburnum davidii* links the garden to the house. **10.** Slender stems of bamboo, *Arundinaria nitida*, create interest from the window without blocking the light. The plants can be thinned to maintain their airy elegance. **11.** *Rodgersia pinnata* has strongly patterned foliage. **12.** With its racemes of yellow flowers, *Mahonia japonica* provides interest in early spring. **13.** Trained against the front wall, *Garrya elliptica* breaks the line of the front elevation.

Paved/shade/winter: 1. The clinging stems of the hydrangea make a marvellous outline against the wall. Plant crocuses at its base. **2.** Yew. **3.** Ivy. **4.** *Daphne* produces perfumed, white flowers in late winter and early spring. **5.** Plant pink and purple hyacinths in the containers. For early winter overplant the bulbs with half-hardy Cape heathers, *Erica gracilis*. **6.** *Fatsia* carries white, candelabra-like flowers well into winter. **7.** Bamboo. **8.** The foliage of the *Elaeagnus* shows up splendidly against the green plants behind. **9.** *Kerria* loses its leaves but retains its elegant stems. **10.** A low container filled with pink, single, early tulips 'Ibis' surrounded by grape hyacinths, *Muscari*. (See page 75 for this garden in summer.)

WINTER

Some winter-flowering shrubs such as viburnums and late-flowering cherries bloom before the middle of winter. Immediately afterwards, depending on aspect and temperature, the first buds of winter jasmine and camellias may start to break, followed by the first snowdrops.

With the possible exception of camellias there are no hard or bright colours, but the subtle shades that do appear are especially rewarding against the bleak backdrop of winter.

More bulbs appear in late winter, including early narcissi 'February Gold', species crocuses and miniature irises.

There are few chores during winter, although the last of the herbaceous plants may need trimming back and fallen leaves must be swept away. It may be necessary to water during dry spells; always check, especially if plants are in the lee of walls or under the overhang of buildings.

Shade: 1. The lime is dormant and can be pruned if ▷ necessary. Official permission may be necessary in urban areas. **2.** Bays tolerate all but the coldest winters. Keep them slightly moist and do not allow them to dry out completely. **3.** Bays. **4.** The evergreen foliage of the *Mahonia* is carried through the winter. **5.** The hydrangeas carry their faded blooms. Tidy the general shapes and leave until spring. **6.** Japanese quinces. **7.** As the leaves of *Schizophragma* fall, the skeleton of the trellis work appears; allow dead flower heads to remain. **8.** Clematis. **9.** The scarlet berries on the *Skimmia japonica* continue into winter. Flower buds formed on *S.* 'Rubella' add interest. **10.** Ivy. **11.** Clear away the leaves as the plantain lilies finally collapse. **12.** Plant winter cherries, *Solanum capsicastrum*, over layers of narcissus bulbs. **13.** For neatness and future bushy growth, cut the fuchsias partially back.

Sun and shade: 1. The wisteria is a hard outline. Now is the time to train it properly and carry out any major pruning. **2.** The first yellow flowers appear on the winter jasmine. **3.** If you were unable to prune the rose in autumn, do so now. **4.** Plant bulbs for spring, including crocuses, single, early tulips, and late-flowering narcissi. Plant miniature irises, narcissi and species tulips along the edge of the path where you can inspect them closely. **5.** *Daphne.* **6.** The Japanese quince first flowers in late winter or early spring. **7.** *Ceanothus.* **8.** *Senecio.* **9.** Plant the central vase with hyacinths for spring. **10.** The lavender maintains its form throughout winter. **11.** The first flowers on the camellia can appear before mid-winter in a mild year and continue into early spring. **12.** Lady's mantle dies back, so remove dead leaves and flowers. **13.** Hellebore's unusual green flowers appear soon after mid-winter.

SPECIAL

Town house: 1. Ground cover of ivy, *Hedera caenwoodiana*. **2.** *Senecio greyi*; stretched by the lower light, its branches weave in and out of the juniper and ivy. **3.** The dominant form of the juniper, *Juniperus* 'Pfitzerana', gives individuality to the planting. **4.** The silver stems of the weeping birch, *Betula pendula* 'Youngii', rise through the green juniper. **5.** Virginia creeper, *Parthenocissus quinquefolia*, is trained to form sheets of green—brilliant crimson in autumn—around the doorway and window.

Above: A formal pattern is created by the brick edging and tiles. Asymmetrical balance comes from major plants, and interest from a miscellany of smaller ones.

Right: Clematis and jasmine soften the red brick walls, while seasonal plants and dwarf perennials provide interest and colour between the irregular paving stones.

Winter continued

Sun: 1. Roses form a dormant framework. **2.** Holly carries its winter berries. **3.** The viburnum has pink buds and blush flowers. **4.** Lavender. **5.** Honeysuckle. **6.** Mexican mock orange. **7.** The hydrangea forms a lattice of dark brown branches against the wall. **8.** *Cotoneaster* carries red berries. **9.** The old leaves of southernwood fall and must be cleared away. **10.** London pride. **11.** The spaces for seasonal planting are now taken up with wallflowers, *Cheiranthus*; forget-me-nots, *Myosotis*; polyanthus, *Primula polyantha*; and daisies, *Bellis*. **12.** Traditional perennials are at a low ebb unless hellebores have been included. **13.** On a sheltered wall, forsythia begins flowering in late winter. **14.** Rosemary adds form to the planting throughout the winter.

Low maintenance/sun: 1. The very large leaves of *Hedera colchica* distinguish it from other ivies. **2.** *Griselinia littoralis* has bright green leaves. **3.** The neat, variegated foliage of *Euonymus radicans* 'Variegatus' covers the soil. **4.** Dwarf bamboos, *Arundinaria variegata*. **5.** The ivy, *Hedera helix* 'Aureovariegata', has soft, yellow and green, irregular markings. **6.** The narrow, dark green leaves and yellow spring flowers of the barberries, *Berberis* x *stenophylla*, form a hedge of arching sprays. **7.** *Cotoneaster salicifolius*, a strong-growing form, has evergreen foliage and red berries. **8.** The large leaves of *Bergenia cordifolia* contrast strongly with the surrounding foliage. **9.** *Mahonia pinnata* soon forms a solid block of attractive foliage with yellow flowers in early summer. **10.** Low, spreading form of common yew, *Taxus* 'Repens'. **11.** Stepping-stones. **12.** Winter jasmine, *Jasminum nudiflorum*, bears bright yellow flowers throughout winter. **13.** Lawn or paving.

Paved/sun/winter: 1. The potato vine loses its leaves. Trim it for winter, and plant bulbs of blue hyacinths at its base. **2.** Myrtle. **3.** Remove cranesbill foliage when it has fully died back. **4.** The bare stems of the broom still provide a green 'break' at the edge of the container. **5.** Plant narcissus 'Peeping Tom' bulbs; winter cherries, *Solanum capsicastrum*, above them provide immediate effect. **6.** As leaf stems of the Chinese fan palm die, cut them off tight to the main stem. **7.** Keep the *Pittosporum* trimmed to restrict its growth. **8.** Remove dead flowers from the *Santolina* and generally trim the plant to keep its shape. **9.** Cut away dead lower leaves on the *Cordyline*, close to the main stem. **10.** A low planter filled with iridescent pinky red tulips 'Toronto'; ivy cushions the edge through winter. (See page 71 for this garden in summer.)

BASEMENTS

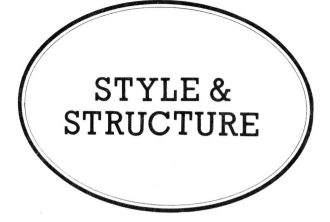
With imagination – and not too much expense – almost any basement area can be transformed into a charming and restful green space.

Areas with direct access from inside can be treated as extensions of the interior. Let the style of the room from which the basement opens be reflected in the garden furniture; or repeat architectural details from doorways or windows on containers for the plants.

If you don't have a door leading to your basement, concentrate on the view from the window. Start by establishing strong, ever-green foliage patterns – particularly on walls visible from the window – that will remain attractive even in winter.

Trellis-work panels, mirrors, pools and fountains, jardinières and sculpture all add a sense of individual style. Lights are effective, especially when contrasted with subdued lighting inside the house. The occasional spotlight directed down from the building or up between the plants can be dramatic.

Sunlight – or lack of it – is a problem. White, cream or pale green walls help to reflect it into the house, and provide a good background for green foliage. A lacy climber on a white wall will allow more light to reach

Left: The bed in this shady basement is dominated by the *Fatsia japonica* and ivy. The winter cherry has grown considerably in this protected environment.

Cobbles or paving stones provide ready-made drainage for plants in pots or tubs.

Grow climbing plants around wooden shutters painted to match a bench or other furniture.

the room than will a densely packed ivy on a darker surface. This conflict between the visual potential of foliage and its effect on the light is inevitable – the final choice is up to you.

When choosing plants, remember that they will naturally be drawn upwards to the higher light source. Select – and manage – them with care, training the leading shoots sideways so that they don't go leggy.

Finally, don't block channels or gutters leading to drains. And remember never to build raised flower beds directly against house or boundary walls.

Paint plain or uninteresting railings a soft colour if you want them to 'disappear'.

Make intricate railings and curved stairs into a positive design feature, using them as the focus for an arrangement of plants.

GREEN SKELETON

Sun

1. The pale green leaves of *Pittosporum tenuifolium* fill the corner. Virginia creeper, *Parthenocissus henryana*, clings to the wall. **2.** *Vitis vinifera* 'Brandt' covers the pergola, and may produce bunches of small, black grapes in this sunny position. Plant in the ground to encourage fruiting. If you decide on a container, use the front for a seasonal planting. **3.** The European fan palm, *Chamaerops humilis*. **4.** *Yucca filamentosa* produces a strong foliage pattern with spikes of cream flowers in summer. **5.** The broom, *Cytisus* x *praecox*, maintains its green form all year and has cream flowers in early summer. **6.** The camellia, *C.* x *williamsii* 'J. C. Williams', can bear blush-pink flowers throughout a good winter. **7.** Seasonal plantings.

Shade

1. *Cotoneaster salicifolius* underplanted with *Muehlenbeckia complexa*, which also climbs on the wall. **2.** The yew, *Taxus* 'Repens', cushions the front of the container; the dainty ivy, *Hedera helix* 'Silver Queen', is behind. **3.** *Fatsia japonica*. Cut back some main stems each spring to encourage bushy lower growth. **4.** Clematis, *C. armandii*, frames the seat. It bears white flowers in spring. **5.** The dark green foliage and red flower buds of *Skimmia* 'Rubella' contrast with: **6.** The pale, bright green of *Griselinia littoralis*. **7.** *Pieris taiwanensis*; flowers similar to lilies of the valley give way to bronze, young foliage in spring. **8.** Seasonal plantings.

Sun

Shade

DARK

Contrasting foliage is more important than flowers in shaded basements: evergreens to provide interest during winter, ferns and other pale-leaved plants for a subtle, atmospheric effect in summer. White or pale cream walls are an effective foil for leaf patterns, and also reflect light.

Durable busy Lizzie is one of the few flowers worth using. Bulbs will always bear elongated plants, so choose the shortest possible varieties.

Rectangular: 1. Shade-loving plants, all of which need ▷ moisture: broad-leaved *Rheum, Hosta, Rodgersia*; ferns *Osmunda, Phyllitis, Pteridium; Cyperus vegetus* with fine, upright foliage; and bamboo, *Arundinaria nitida*. **2.** A fibreglass boulder with interior light. **3.** Side walls are clad in creeping fig, *Ficus pumila*. This is suitable only for warmer areas. An ivy, *Hedera*, would be suitable for cooler spots. **4.** A permanently fixed, sprinkler hose connects to a flexible hose near the window or some other convenient point, for easier watering. **5.** The mural provides year-round interest, and an alternative pattern during winter. **6.** Ground cover of *Helxine soleirolii* around the boulder.

Informal: 1. Bamboo, *Arundinaria nitida,* and golden privet, *Ligustrum* 'Aureum'. Keep the latter pruned, but not trimmed, to maintain shape and produce pleasant lime-green foliage. **2.** Tub containing a 'lace-cap' hydrangea, *H.* 'Blue Wave', which flowers from late summer; and a type of Virginia creeper, *Parthenocissus henryana*. The latter clings to the wall. **3.** The Portugal laurel, *Prunus lusitanica*, has good evergreen foliage. **4.** Strongly patterned, evergreen shrubs such as *Mahonia* or *Aucuba*, and climbing plants. **5.** Old conservatory staging with individual pots of seasonal flowers. Cineraria or polyanthus, *Primula polyantha*, are good choices for spring. Summer plants include: fuchsias; busy Lizzie, *Impatiens*; flame nettles, *Coleus*; and *Asparagus sprengeri*. **6.** Seat.

Smaller terracotta pots beside **1** contain seasonal plants; African lilies, *Agapanthus*; or herbs. Containers for plantings **1** to **4** are painted to match.

Low maintenance: 1. A large planter contains a multi-stemmed silver birch, *Betula alba*, formed by planting three or four small trees together. This is underplanted with x *Fatshedera lizei* which maintains its evergreen foliage when the birch is leafless. **2.** Allow the regal fern, *Osmunda regalis*, a whole container so that it can achieve its full potential. The odd plant of small-leaved ivy, *Hedera helix* 'Jubilee', will break the line of the vase during winter. **3.** The arching branches of the quince, *Chaenomeles speciosa* 'Rosea Plena', are left untrained and give shape to the tall container. **4.** Plant two units with busy Lizzie, *Impatiens sultanii*, for summer colour. **5.** The cut-leafed sumac, *Rhus typhina* 'Laciniata', is underplanted with *Bergenia cordifolia*. **6.** Built-in seat. **7.** Wall sculpture.

There are no climbing plants, which need constant care, in this easily maintained garden.

◁ **Formal: 1.** Summer plantings of busy Lizzie, *Impatiens*, and fuchsias. **2.** The variegated hollies, *Ilex* x *altaclarensis* 'Golden King', have bright foliage throughout the year and can be clipped to shape. **3.** Climbing plants at both ends of side walls. Choose from the glory vine, *Vitis coignetiae*; the golden hop, *Humulus lupulus* 'Aureus'; and ivy, *Hedera colchica*. The hop is cut down to base each year, encouraging lower growth. **4.** Trailing plants for the edges of the raised planting boxes are green ivy, *Hedera helix* 'Chicago'; periwinkle, *Vinca minor*, would also be suitable. **5.** Seat. **6.** Choose from the Japanese anemones, *Anemone japonica*; *Tradescantia virginiana*; plantain lilies, *Hosta*; hardy ferns—*Asplenium*, *Phyllitis* or *Pteridium*; and *Pachysandra terminalis*.

CHILDREN AND BASEMENTS

It can be difficult to provide playing space for young, active children in a small basement. However, a few games can be built into your plan, even in this tiny area.

For toddlers, a sandbox at one end can give hours of pleasure, with the added benefit of fresh air. Build it across the end, but be sure to provide protection for the walls on three sides. Lay a length of strong, heavy rubber or plastic lining under the box and run it at least 6in. (15cm) up the sides to prevent any damp retained in the sand from penetrating the walls. When the children are older, convert the box into a garden specially for them – and later into a fern garden for yourself.

A hopscotch grid can be painted on tiles or linoleum with plastic paint, and an open-bottomed, net basket for ball games can be attached to one of the longer walls where two or three children can reach it from the sides as well as the front. A dart board (for use with rubber-tipped darts) can be hung on a short wall. All these can be easily removed when children grow up.

A small, folding table and chairs will be convenient for drawing, painting and playing card or paper games in good weather – one advantage of a basement area is that it is unlikely to be windy.

LIGHT

Even in a light basement at least one wall will always be in shade. The height of the walls also affects the amount of light available.

The natural source of light will encourage plants to reach upwards – even if the walls are white. Train climbing varieties sideways to cover part of the walls before reaching the top.

Use shrubs for partial shade. In summer, busy Lizzie and fuchsias will probably be more successful than petunias or geraniums.

Roses: 1. The climbing rose 'Mermaid' is trained over the doorway on to trellis panels which reflect and emphasize the pattern of the raised bed. **2.** Wall plaque. **3.** Raised bed. It must have adequate drainage. The edging of Christmas box, *Sarcococca humilis*, forms an evergreen band through winter. **4.** Roses for the border and wall. Some possibilities are: 'Cecile Brunner', with small, pale yellow flowers shading to rose pink; 'Iceberg', a white floribunda; and 'All Gold', a bright yellow floribunda. Appropriate climbing roses include: 'Zéphirine Drouhin', a thornless, fragrant, bright pink; and 'Étoile de Hollande', a fragrant, dark red rose. **5.** Corner groups of standard, half-standard, and bush roses, arranged to form pyramid shapes. Choose colours that blend with the climbing roses. **6.** Seat.

Informal: 1. Stand flowering plants on the table. **2.** Corner units with the cream broom, *Cytisus x praecox*, and a vine, *Vitis vinifera* 'Brandt'; and *Senecio greyi* and the evergreen honeysuckle, *Lonicera halleana*. **3.** The autumn-flowering cherry, *Prunus subhirtella* 'Autumnalis Rosea', has pink flowers during winter. The honey locust, *Gleditsia triacanthos* 'Sunburst' has bright yellow foliage throughout summer. Both trees can be pruned to keep them from shielding the sun. **4.** Seasonal plantings. Plant narcissi, tulips and hyacinths for spring. Possibilities for summer include alyssum and tobacco plants, *Nicotiana*. **5.** Deep but narrow boxes house climbing plants: possibilities include early flowering clematis, *C. armandii*; and early Dutch and late Dutch honeysuckles, *Lonicera periclymenum* 'Belgica' and *L. periclymenum* 'Serotina'. **6.** Half-baskets contain trailing fuchsias and ivy-leaved geraniums, *Pelargonium peltatum*, for summer colour.

Low maintenance: 1. *Arundinaria murieliae*, a slender-stemmed bamboo. **2.** *Mahonia pinnata* forms a mound of evergreen foliage with yellow flowers in late spring. **3.** Prune back the new growth of the glory vine, *Vitis coignetiae*, each winter so that trails of new foliage hang down the sides of the pot. **4.** A bowl of *Azalea* 'Palestrina', with white flowers among its semi-evergreen foliage in late spring. A tap for watering is behind it. **5.** Mobile barbecue. **6.** Benches on castors for sun-bathing or eating. **7.** The African lily, *Agapanthus*, has blue flower spikes during summer and attractive, strap-like foliage through part of winter. **8.** The mallow, *Lavatera olbia*, produces cerise pink flowers all summer. Trim it back in spring to keep its shape. **9.** Prune back the gum tree, *Eucalyptus gunnii*, in spring to encourage new, silver growth.

◁ **Formal: 1.** Camellias, *C.* x *williamsii* 'Donation', are pinned to walls. They should be well-mulched and fed after flowering in early summer. **2.** The main frame-works of *Escallonia* 'Apple Blossom' are trained to the walls, while short, flowering branches come forward to create a softer effect. **3.** Summer jasmine, *Jasminum officinale*, with its evening perfume, grows on the sunny trellises. Train the shrubs across the doorway. **4a.** Bowls contain summer plantings of sun-loving plants like geraniums (zonal pelargoniums) or petunias. **4b.** Bowls at the shady end hold half-hardy fuchsias; busy Lizzies *Impatiens sultanii*; and begonias. **5.** Seat. **6.** Plants tumbling over the edges of the boxes include brooms, *Genista lydia* and *Cytisus kewensis*, near the sunny end; *Cotoneaster dammeri* in the centre; and ivy, *Hedera*, in the shade. **7.** Plantings include lady's mantle, *Alchemilla mollis*; flag iris, *I. pallida*; and *Sedum* x 'Autumn Joy'.

Useful: 1. Train Morello cherries, *Prunus cerasus* 'Morello', along wires. The formal shape of the branches will provide winter interest when the trees are dormant. **2, 3.** Use east- and west-facing walls for plants which need more sun: green beans; peaches, *Prunus persica*; or thornless blackberries, *Rubus fruticosus* 'Oregon Thornless'. **4.** Take advantage of the full south-facing position to grow tomatoes. Try different types including the small, red 'Cherry' and yellow 'Plum'. **5.** Terracotta half-pots or other lower tubs contain herbs. **6.** A mop-headed bay, *Laurus nobilis*, is at the base of the steps.

VISUAL EFFECTS

Random planting creates its own quite acceptable design, but you may want a more ordered, architectural effect. At its simplest, this stems from a geometrical lay-out of beds or carefully selected containers. Trellis work and mirrors can be used to additional effect.

Although plants are still an essential element, they generally emphasize formality.

Classic: 1. Mop-headed bays, *Laurus nobilis*, in ▷ panelled tubs (*caisses Versailles*). **2.** Simple boxes with training frames on wall above. The dark green ivy, *Hedera helix* 'Chicago', follows the lines of the frames. **3.** Seat; the simple wooden frame above it breaks the wall visually. Seat, frames, and tubs are painted the same colour. **4.** A single classic vase for an appropriate summer planting: geraniums (zonal pelargoniums) for sunny positions, fuchsias or busy Lizzie, *Impatiens*, for shade. **5.** Gravel can camouflage an old basement floor where there is no foot traffic, but be sure to place mesh over drain outlets to prevent blockage.

Wall fountain: 1. A fountain consisting of a wall mask, an intermediate bowl and a pool. A re-circulating pump in the pool delivers water to the mask via a pipe buried in the wall. **2.** Fine rope passed through screw-eyes forms arches. **3.** Simple, square pots painted to match wall or floor contain *Hedera helix* 'Glacier' for the arches. **4.** Formal plants in terracotta pots centred in each arch—choose from bay, *Laurus nobilis*; yew, *Taxus*; holly, *Ilex*; or the dwarf cypress, *Chamaecyparis lawsoniana* 'Ellwoodii'. **5.** A lower bed can be extended from the base of the pool; edge with periwinkles, *Vinca minor*.

'Japanese': 1. Raised beds retained by wooden boards. **2.** Slotted platform with bonsai trees. **3.** Slats continue up the wall to form a vertical plant support for *Muehlenbeckia complexa*. **4.** An upright-growing Japanese maple, *Acer palmatum* 'Osakazuki'. **5.** Low-growing, spreading Japanese maples, such as *Acer palmatum* 'Dissectum Viridis'. **6.** Lantern. **7.** The pine, *Pinus mugo* 'Muga', is of dwarf, rounded habit. **8.** Low plants and gravel between specimen plants from the following list: the creeping dogwood *Cornus canadensis*; Christmas box, *Sarcococca*; and bugle plants, *Ajuga reptans*.

◁ **Trellis and mirror: 1.** An end mirror, with perspective trellis radiating from it, reflects the large vase and 'extends' the courtyard. Creeping fig, *Ficus pumila*, frames the mirror and covers parts of the perspective trellis. **2.** Side mirrors set behind simpler trellis, also with creeping fig. The central vase is reflected in the 'windows'. **3.** Corner boxes contain climbing plants: clematis, *C. armandii* and *C. tangutica*; and wisteria, *Wistaria sinensis*. The flowers are mirrored in the glass. **4.** Central vase contains summer planting of busy Lizzie, *Impatiens*.

Sculptural: 1. Steps and wall painted to look like a piece of sculpture. **2.** Simple tub contains privet, *Ligustrum lucidum*. **3.** Railings are painted soft blue-green to 'disappear'. **4.** Low planter with a single species of ground cover, *Pachysandra terminalis*, which provides a foil for the sculpture. **5.** Simple containers with 'sculptural' plants: Sumac, *Rhus typhina* 'Laciniata', has large, heavily 'cut' leaves; *Stephanandra incisa* has attractive, low, arching foliage; Mexican mock orange, *Choisya ternata*, has rounded, bright green foliage.

TERRACES

One way of bringing light into basement rooms is to demolish the vertical walls opposite the house and replace them with a stepped-back garden. A successful conversion will provide space for plants, a series of safe steps to the lower level – and a pleasing view from the house.

Even a very simple garden must have proper retaining walls, and an adequate depth of soil. The surface of the latter must be slightly below the tops of the walls to prevent erosion as the water runs off the beds.

Terracing: Terracing a slope is an ancient but none- ▷ theless effective way of controlling soil erosion and providing level growing beds in which plants can establish themselves easily. A small terraced area could be covered, easily and strikingly, with an all-over planting of the same ground-cover plant. The structure of the terracing could be brick, block, or secondhand timber.

Be prepared to spend most of your money on plants. Many specimens of the plant you choose must be planted quite close together in order to achieve full cover quickly. A single, sculptured tree and climbing plants for the side trellis will create simple and striking relief, but the scheme relies on the overall leaf texture of the ground cover. For a sunny area choose rose of Sharon, *Hypericum calycinum*; roses, *Rosa* 'Max Graff'; or *Rubus tricolor*. For a shady area try periwinkles, *Vinca major* or *Cotoneaster* 'Skogsholm'.

Cercis siliquastrum is a good choice for the tree. Ivy, *Hedera colchica*, is a fine climber in the shade, and *Actinidia kolomikta* is good in the sun.

Stepped garden/sun: 1. *Buddleia alternifolia*, trained as a small tree, has long, drooping branches laden with pale blue flowers in summer. **2.** The grey leaves of *Senecio greyi* withstand traffic dirt. **3.** *Convolvulus cneorum* has silver-grey foliage and white flowers throughout summer. **4.** *Kolkwitzia amabilis*, if kept in bounds, makes a delightful, summer-flowering shrub with soft pink flowers. **5.** The strong foliage pattern of *Mahonia lomariifolia* creates interest in winter; it also flowers in early spring. **6.** Roses and clematis cover the trellis. **7.** *Magnolia grandiflora* trained over a larger wall area and onto the face of the house, bears cream-white flowers in summer. **8.** *Cotoneaster* 'Autumn Fire' has arching stems and berries in autumn. **9.** Herbaceous plants include *Nerine bowdenii*; iris, *I. sibirica*; *Geum*; and *Euphorbia polychroma*. Edging plants are candytuft, *Iberis*; and London pride, *Saxifraga umbrosa*.

Stepped garden/shade: 1. *Gleditsia* 'Sunburst', a small light foliage tree. **2.** The medium-size evergreen shrub *Cotoneaster salicifolius floccosus* gives some seclusion from passers-by. **3.** A Japanese azalea in your choice of colour cushions the corner. **4.** *Kerria japonica* 'Variegata' has arching stems with dainty, variegated foliage. **5.** The dark green, evergreen *Prunus laurocerasus* 'Otto Luyken'. **6.** Ivy, *Hedera colchica*, and a hydrangea, *H. petiolaris*, cover the wall and trellis. **7.** Fuchsia 'Versicolor' has arching, variegated foliage. **8.** An assortment of herbaceous plants among the shrubs: plantain lilies, *Hosta*; *Bergenia*; and day lilies, *Hemerocallis*. The edging is *Mimulus* and bellflowers, *Campanula*. **9.** Window box.

◁ **Conversion/sun: 1.** Weeping pear, *Pyrus salicifolia.* **2.** *Potentilla fruticosa* 'Katherine Dykes' is in the corner; Jerusalem sage, *Phlomis fruticosa,* across the front edge. **3.** Winter jasmine, *Jasminum nudiflorum,* is next to the entrance; you will pass it each day. **4.** Variegated ivy, *Hedera colchica dentata* 'Aurea', forms a year-round screen. **5.** *Daphne retusa* has fragrant flowers in early summer. **6.** The compact mock orange, *Philadelphus* 'Manteau d'Hermine', is backed by honeysuckle, *Lonicera fuchsoides,* on the trellis. **7.** *Hebe* 'Autumn Glory' has blue flowers in late summer. **8.** Vases on small platforms can be used for seasonal plantings. (See 'Informal', page 92.) Or use plants with strong foliage patterns—*Yucca* or African lilies, *Agapanthus* —or soft, trailing plants like catmint, *Nepeta;* and clematis, *C. alpina.*

Conversion/shade: 1. The autumn-flowering cherry, *Prunus subhirtella* 'Autumnalis Rosea', flowers blush pink throughout winter. **2.** *Desfontaina spinosa* can easily be kept in shape; it bears scarlet, tubular flowers in late summer. **3.** The quince, *Chaenomeles speciosa* 'Nivalis', has white flowers in early spring. It is trained against the wall and tied into the railing. **4.** The ivy, *Hedera* 'Emerald Green', is one of the few climbers that is tough enough for this aspect. **5.** The leathery foliage of *Viburnum davidii* creates a year-round foil to the steps and brickwork. **6.** The ornamental flowering currant, *Ribes* 'Brocklebankii', has pink flowers in spring; the leaves that follow will probably be lime-green in this position, rather than their usual golden-yellow. *Schizophragma hydrangeoides* grows on the fence. **7.** *Euonymus radicans* 'Variegatus' provides a soft mound of cushioning foliage. **8.** Seasonal plantings of busy Lizzie, *Impatiens,* or half-hardy fuchsias in the vases; or trailing plants in the tall, oil jars—Virginia creeper, *Parthenocissus,* would be ideal.

SIDE PASSAGEWAYS

Left: Stacking units clad the wall and give growing space for a range of herbs, ivies and ferns.

STYLE & STRUCTURE

Walls, fences and hedges dominate this chapter. Because they almost always create a funnelling or shading effect, conditions are often the worst possible for establishing plants.

Paint or trellises, geometric or romantic, can be effective: even a gloomy passageway becomes attractive if the walls are white, pink or apricot, and if pots flank the door and plants scramble over the trellis work. In shady areas overhung by trees, set green trellises against white walls.

Side passages are all too often the route for drains and sewers. Faced with 'wall to wall' concrete left by an unfeeling builder or developer, you may be limited to using containers for all your plants. However, try to establish them in the ground wherever possible – they will thrive and be easier to keep.

Choose plants that will withstand adverse conditions and stay neat and tidy – especially if the area is your only access to a back garden. They will automatically stretch upwards to reach the light, so it is essential that sun-loving plants at ground level are trimmed and cut back to promote bushy growth at the base.

Cushioning plants at the base of a wall or fence can often serve a dual purpose if you also train them upwards by tying them back to a wire frame or trellis.

When planting, always remember to leave a 4in. to 6in. (about 10cm to 15cm) space between the plants and the wall; otherwise

Shortened paving stones provide space for plants. Trellis panels can be painted to lighten the area.

Plants in pots and window boxes will emphasize the door and windows, disguise the end enclosure.

Passage with rustic-style gate. Establish plants along side and train climbers along wires.

Leave space between plants and the house wall so that roots can be thoroughly watered.

Trellis and alcoves create an ideal setting for a formal plan; the brickwork adds emphasis.

Paving emphasizes perspective. Train climbers along the walls and make a feature of the dead-end.

their roots may become dry, even in the shade, before they are established.

Avoid using plants with long internodal growth in heavily shaded areas – honeysuckles, for example, will become drawn and unhappy.

Moss softens the appearance of paving stones, but can be slippery and dangerous on certain natural stone surfaces. Your choice of low, spreading plants to grow in paving cracks will be determined by the amount of light that reaches the ground. Try *Helxine soleirolii*, a small-leaved ivy or bellflowers, *Campanula poscharskyana*, in shade; sweet Williams, pinks or wild thyme in the sun.

Take advantage of sunlit gates and fences and paint them in strong primary colours to contrast with the delicacy of foliage.

Shade

Sun

This plan, like the one for shady areas, is composed of three elements: wall shrubs or climbers; cushioning plants which visually link the walls to the ground; and plants that will cover or soften the edges of the paving material.

1. Slats painted pale and dark blue. **2.** *Actinidia kolomikta* has dark green leaves with pale pink and cream tips. **3.** Pale blue flag irises, *Iris germanica*, bloom in spring. **4.** *Alchemilla conjuncta*; leave it to spread and self-seed. **5.** *Senecio greyi* is trained onto the wall, but also left as a bush at the base. It bears yellow flowers in summer. **6.** Spaces for seasonal plantings.

Shade

1. Ivy, *Hedera helix* 'Jubilee'. **2.** The climbing hydrangea, *H. petiolaris*, has cream-white flowers in early summer. **3.** Christmas box, *Sarcococca humilis*, forms a neat, rounded shape at the foot of the wall. **4.** *Euonymus radicans* 'Variegatus'. **5.** *Garrya elliptica*. **6.** Persian ivy, *H. colchica*. **7.** Spaces for seasonal plantings.

Side areas fall into two categories: passageways and dead-ends.

By providing a proper door (with an efficient door closer) in passageways some draughts – the main threat to plants in these areas – can be eliminated. Even a fine mesh of trellis work will reduce the impact of the wind – and may be better than a solid form around which the wind eddies.

Stagger containers to give enough space for people to pass by them. Choose tough plants that will survive constant traffic.

Dead-ends are best treated as elongated, and often shady, courtyards. The solid barrier at one end prevents draughts, and also allows you to create a focal point: a vase on a pedestal, a mirror (lead-backed to prevent deterioration of the silvering), a tree or a grouping of plants. Lay paving so that it leads the eye to this central feature.

Alternatively, the barrier could be the site for rubbish containers, disguised with trellis panels, or for the repetition of an architectural detail.

Passage: 1. Wisteria, *Wistaria sinensis*, has attractive summer foliage, preceded by drooping mauve flowers. **2.** *Nerine bowdenii* has strap-like foliage, with spikes carrying pink flowers through late summer. **3.** Christmas box, *Sarcococca humilis*, has evergreen foliage, with perfumed flowers in late winter. **4.** The glory vine, *Vitis coignetiae*, covers the wall with its large, architectural leaves. Tie in shoots, and limit top growth. The vine provides superb autumn colour. **5.** Seasonal plantings. **6.** The trellis panels are detachable. **7.** Alternate paving stones are shortened to make planting pockets.

Practical: 1. Roof of corrugated plastic. Make sure the material is fire-resistant, and check whether official planning permission is required. **2.** End trellis panel. **3.** Enclosure for rubbish. Children's bicycles could be slung from hooks above the enclosure, large cycles stored between the panel and the bins. Clean, flat plastic backing on the panel and end gate, **4**, together with the plastic roof, will keep out the worst of the weather. But cycles do tend to deteriorate under these conditions. **5.** Window box. **6.** Evergreen, climbing plant in a large vase, or set directly into the ground. **7.** Vase. Choose tough plants like *Aucuba* and ivy, *Hedera*, that will survive under the roof.

Dead-end: 1. Bay trees, *Laurus nobilis*, in terracotta pots. **2.** Boxes contain grey *Helichrysum petiolatum*; lemon-coloured French marigolds, *Tagetes patula;* and white petunias. **3.** These plantings are reflected in the containers on top of the dustbin. **4.** Details on the door, box supports and canopy are similar. **5.** The bamboo, *Arundinaria nitida*, breaks the corner lines but allows access to bins. **6.** The camellia, *C. x williamsii* 'St. Ewe', has pink flowers in early spring, and can be trained to the wall. **7.** Low planting includes *Viburnum davidii, Tradescantia virginiana* and Japanese anemones, *A. japonica*. **8.** If the area is reasonably draught-free, clematis, *C. armandii*, evergreen with small white flowers, is a good choice.

Passage: 1. The yellow-berried firethorn, *Pyracantha rogersiana* 'Flavia', is trained along horizontal wires. There may be fewer flowers and less fruit as it moves away from the sun. **2.** The Japanese quince, *Chaenomeles* x *Superba* 'Knap Hill Scarlet', has bright orange-red flowers on leafless stems during spring. **3.** *Garrya eliptica* has interesting catkins in spring. **4.** *Cotoneaster horizontalis* can grow against the walls and also spread out across the paving. **5.** Allow small, hardy ferns—*Asplenium*, *Phyllitis* or *Pteridium*—to naturalize. **6.** *Helxine soleirolii* fills cracks between paving stones.

Passage: 1. Structural planting includes ivy, *Hedera helix* 'Chicago', trailing over the front, *Aucuba japonica*, *Skimmia* 'Rubella' and *Euonymus fortunei* 'Silver Queen'. **2.** A single pot contains narcissi 'Silver Chimes' in spring; busy Lizzie, *Impatiens*, in summer; ivy, *Hedera helix*, makes a foliage break on the trellis. **3.** x *Fatshedera lizei* has an unusual, semi-rigid form; tie its main leaders onto wires which stretch across the alcoves. **4.** The alcove is reflected in a mirror. A wall planter is positioned above the reflection. **5.** Trellis work. **6.** The pattern made by the bricks emphasizes the alcoves.

Dead-end: 1. The honey locust, *Gleditsia triacanthos* 'Sunburst', has delicate, lime-green to yellow foliage. **2.** *Mahonia japonica* has distinctive, evergreen foliage and racemes of lemon yellow flowers in late winter. **3.** *Pieris* 'Forest Flame' produces brilliantly coloured young foliage in late spring. **4.** The self-clinging hydrangea, *H. petiolaris*, has flat, 'lace-cap' flowers held horizontally. **5.** Pots of plantain lilies, *Hosta glauca*. **6.** The yellow flowers of the clematis, *C. orientalis*, appear in early autumn and are followed by attractive seed heads. **7.** *Rodgersia* produces strongly patterned foliage during summer.

Dead-end: 1. The vase on the tall pedestal is filled with a summer planting. An ideal combination would be trailing, half-hardy fuchsias in cerise and deep purple, and bellflowers, *Campanula isophylla*. **2.** Periwinkle, *Vinca major*, makes a green base for the plinth. **3.** The long fronds of *Pteridium* add softness during summer. **4.** The ivy, *Hedera helix* 'Aureovariegata', has year-round, green foliage with a subtle hint of pale green and yellow. **5.** Paving emphasizes perspective. **6.** The rose 'Mermaid' is allowed to scramble to the light, then falls from the top of the wall carrying its single cream/yellow flowers.

BALCONIES

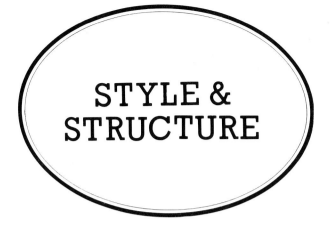

STYLE & STRUCTURE

Simple, small, window balcony. Keep front plants low to allow light into the room.

A balcony garden can be practical (framing or obliterating a view, or screening you from your neighbours) or aesthetic (simply providing an attractive annex to a living room). In both cases the position of the containers is vital. Decide on this from inside the room, or you may find you've created a garden exclusively for the benefit of others.

As with basements, the style of the room from which the balcony opens can be echoed in containers and/or furniture. Trellis work, floor surfaces and furniture all have a part to play but are basically embellishments in a confined space. While they may add to the overall effect, nothing can replace the grace, vigour and continual interest of a well-designed planting scheme.

Weight is an essential consideration. Most balconies can sustain 30lb to 40lb per square foot (about 13.5kg to 18kg per 0.09 square metres), which means containers can be up to 12in. or 15in. (30cm to 38cm) deep. However, many balconies are cantilevered and cannot take such a large load. Don't exacerbate the problem by placing too many containers along the outer edge.

You will always have to find the right balance between weight and capacity – the larger the container, the better the plants will perform.

Make full use of this balcony with trees in tubs and containers on the balustrade.

Left: Plants in tubs, baskets and boxes bring colour to this recessed balcony.

Brighten a recessed balcony with climbers, and plants in boxes on its outer edge.

Make sure that boxes on parapet walls and railings are properly secured by wire or by screws to well-designed, strong brackets; and never put anything on the floor that could block or interrupt the flow of water to the drain. Install a tap on the balcony if you can – it will save you the effort of carrying water to the containers, and make watering almost a pleasure.

A delightful fantasy will suit this style. Remember to secure containers carefully.

Classic window balcony. Use plants in colours that complement the stained glass.

Sun

106

GREEN SKELETON

Sun

1. *Ceanothus* x *veitchianus* has bright blue flowers in early summer. Alternatively, plant *C.* x 'Autumnal Blue' for a longer flowering season. **2.** Daisy bushes, *Olearia* x *haastii*, have neat, evergreen foliage, and white, daisy-like flowers in summer. **3.** Bear's breeches, *Acanthus mollis*, provide a strong foliage pattern at the base of the arrangement. **4.** Brooms, *Genista lydia*, produce strings of yellow flowers along green, arching stems in late spring and early summer. **5.** *Senecio monroi* has interesting grey leaves with white undersides, and yellow flowers in summer. **6.** *Hebe* 'Autumn Glory' has blue flowers in early autumn; purple-tinted, dark green foliage creates an effective year-round display. **7.** Spaces for seasonal plantings.

Shade

1. Male forms of *Garrya elliptica*, which produce beautiful catkins in early spring, are trained back against the wall. **2.** *Camellia* x *williamsii* produces pink flowers – throughout winter in good years. **3.** *Mahonia pinnata* has sea-green prickly leaves, and yellow flowers in spring. **4.** *Skimmia* 'Rubella', in the centre of the box; crimson buds appear in late autumn, opening to form white flowers in spring. **5.** Variegated *Euonymus radicans* 'Variegatus'. **6.** Christmas box, *Sarcococca humilis*, provides alternative foliage forms. **7.** Spaces for seasonal plantings.

Shade

SPRING

Virtually an extension to a room, a balcony can provide a year-round display of colour and greenery. Short narcissi 'February Gold', short, multi-headed tulips, and crocuses produce splashes of colour from early spring, planted among evergreens which may also have early flowers.

Polyanthus and forget-me-nots flower later, when the narcissi can be replaced by cinerarias, calceolarias and other seasonal plants.

Water boxes well from early spring.

Sun: 1. The autumn-flowering cherry, *Prunus subhirtella* 'Autumnalis Rosea', makes a good, small tree in a tub or deep box; it produces flowers from midwinter with its main flush in early spring. **2.** Variegated ivy, *Hedera helix* 'Glacier', gives the boxes a green façade all year round. **3.** Multi-headed, small narcissi 'Cheerfulness' are pleasantly perfumed. **4.** Single, early tulips in your choice of colour. **5.** The hardy fruiting vine, *Vitis vinifera* 'Brandt', is dormant. **6.** Permanent plantings of rosemary, *Rosmarinus officinalis*; lavender, *Lavandula*; or a *Hebe*. **7.** The evergreen clematis, *C. armandii*, grows from the same container as the tree. It has small, white flowers in early spring. The top of the balustrade is covered with netting to allow the clematis to scramble.

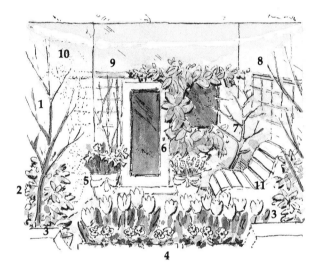

Shade: 1. The false acacia trees, *Robinia pseudoacacia* 'Frisia', remain dormant. **2.** Golden hollies, *Ilex* x *altaclarensis* 'Golden King', give a bright, evergreen effect. **3.** Plantain lilies, *Hosta glauca*, are dormant. **4.** Boxes attached to the wall are filled with mid-season tulips in your choice of colour. Underplant them with pale blue pansies, *Viola* x *wittrockiana*. **5.** The clematis, *C.* 'Nelly Moser', is a dormant framework; allow early narcissi, 'March Sunshine', to naturalize at its base. **6.** Persian ivy, *Hedera colchica*, has large, green leaves; grape hyacinths, *Muscari*, are naturalized at its base. **7.** The cut-leaf sumac, *Rhus typhina* 'Laciniata', is dormant but provides a sculptured framework. **8.** Trellis. **9.** A connecting rail links the tops of the trellis panels. **10.** A complete wall is mirrored for dramatic effect. **11.** Seat.

Sun: 1. Carefully controlled groups of candytuft, *Iberis*, soften corners. Other areas are left free to show the ornamental cast-iron work. **2.** Boxes, painted in a contrasting colour, highlight the ironwork. **3.** Tall, early-flowering, small-flowered narcissi, 'Cheerfulness' for example. **4.** Short, mid-season, small-flowered narcissi. Remove all narcissi when they die back. **5.** Wallflowers, *Cheiranthus*, produce a wide colour range in late spring and create a soft effect around the ironwork.

SPECIAL

Low maintenance/sun: 1. Spanish gorse, *Genista hispanica*, forms a neat line of bright green foliage. Clip into shape in late spring when yellow flowers finish. **2.** *Actinidia kolomikta*, a highly ornamental vine, has green and creamy white leaves; white flowers appear in early summer.

SPECIAL

Low maintenance/shade: 1. *Lonicera pileata* has horizontally formed branches with bright green leaves. In the spring, young foliage appears among the old, creating a dappled effect. **2.** An unusual ivy, *Hedera* 'Cristata', with crinkled, rounded leaves.

SUMMER

By early summer the fresh colours of spring begin to give way to pinks, scarlets and purples, while evergreens take on a new lease of life.

With balcony boxes, unlike window boxes which tumble forward to give the best display to the outsider, it should be possible to encourage some of the plants to face inwards. Train them rigorously or they will face the light source.

As always, boxes and other containers must be regularly watered.

Sun: 1. Light foliage on the cherry tree allows the sun ▷ into the room. **2.** The ivy is at its showiest, covered with new growth. **3, 4.** Bulbs have been removed and boxes are planted with a classic combination of pale pink and pale mauve ivy-leaved geraniums, *Pelargonium* 'Galilee' and *P.* 'La France', mixed with upright geraniums, *P.* 'Paul Crampel' (zonal). **5.** The vine has green foliage. **6.** Safeguard your permanent plants from encroaching seasonal ones and give them enough space to develop properly. **7.** Trim and tidy the clematis after flowering; it must be kept moist if new growth is to be encouraged throughout summer.

Shade: 1. The false acacias have interesting, lime-green foliage throughout summer. **2.** The golden hollies spread broad, green leaves with golden margins. **3.** The plantain lilies have bold, blue-green leaves and whitish flower spikes. **4.** Boxes contain busy Lizzie, *Impatiens sultanii*, in a mixture of deep and pale pinks. **5.** The clematis has pale mauve-pink flowers with a carmine bar. Trim back flowering growths immediately after flowering. **6.** The large, green leaves of the Persian ivy frame the edge of the window. **7.** The sumac has large, fern-like leaves. **8.** Trellis. **9.** Connecting rail. **10.** Mirrored wall. **11.** Seat.

Sun: 1. When the candytuft has flowered in early summer, trim it to maintain a neat shape. **2.** Boxes. **3.** Groups of *Ballota pseudo-dictamnus* produce a grey-green foil for: **4.** White petunias, which scramble happily around the intricate ironwork. They tend to fade in late summer, and their stems become long and stringy. Remove them and fill the gaps with pot-grown chrysanthemums. **5.** Root space is restricted, so use annual climbing plants to soften the walls: morning glory, *Ipomoea*; or black-eyed Susan, *Thunbergia alata*.

SPECIAL

SPECIAL

Useful/sun: 1. Rosemary, *Rosmarinus officinalis*, is evergreen and also provides dried leaves for cooking. **2.** 'Tiny Tim' tomatoes are happy in window boxes, produce an abundance of tiny salad tomatoes, and need no support. **3.** Rue, *Ruta graveolens*, produces bushy, evergreen, blue-grey foliage. The leaves, fresh or dried, are excellent with rich meats, poultry and fish. **4.** Green beans on cane tripod supports. **5.** Fan-trained peach, *Prunus persica*, against the wall. **6.** Strawberry pot filled with your favourite variety. **7.** A fruiting vine, *Vitis* 'Black Hambourg'. **8.** A series of low boxes contains parsley, *Petroselinum crispum*; chives, *Allium schoenoprasum*; mint, *Mentha*; basil, *Ocimum basilicum*; and chervil, *Anthriscus cerefolium*. **9.** The fig, *Ficus carica* 'Brown Turkey', provides dramatic foliage as well as fruit in summer; its branches create a fine, sculptural effect in winter.

Low maintenance: 1. Green artificial grass. **2.** White cylinders. **3.** Pyramid-shaped trees: bay, *Laurus nobilis*; pyramid holly, *Ilex* 'Pyramidalis'; or yew, *Taxus*. **4.** A rising sun, in crimson paint, picks out the forward slats in the ranch fencing around the balcony.

111

AUTUMN

Elevated and often reasonably protected, balconies provide an environment that allows many summer plants to continue flowering well into autumn – a bonus that is sometimes offset by the resulting lack of room for autumn and winter plantings. Try to make space for these.

The turning leaves of climbing, background plants also provide colour, while the *Hebe* will have started to flower in late summer.

Sun: 1. Cherry foliage turns an attractive yellow before ▷ falling. **2.** The ivy can be trimmed to a neat shape before winter sets in. **3, 4.** Given a good autumn, geraniums often continue in flower through early winter. The only attention they need is regular dead-heading, feeding and watering. **5.** The vine has clusters of sweet, aromatic grapes; its leaves turn dark red and purple. **6.** Make sure seasonal plants do not cover the permanent ones. **7.** Any very long growths on the clematis must be 'trained in' onto the net.

Shade: 1. The lime-green foliage of the false acacias turns golden-yellow. **2.** The hollies will probably bear large, red berries. **3.** The leaves of the plantain lilies begin to turn yellow. Remove them when they are completely dead. **4.** Busy Lizzie will survive a mild autumn, but if there are early frosts you may have to replace the plants with dwarf chrysanthemums to maintain colour. **5.** In early autumn, following a second crop of flowers on the clematis, trim the flowering shoots to keep the plant in shape. **6.** Ivy. **7.** The leaves of the sumac turn orange, yellow and red. **8.** Trellis. **9.** Connecting rail. **10.** Mirrored wall. **11.** Seat.

Sun: 1. Candytuft. **2.** Boxes. **3.** *Ballota* continues into autumn, increasing in size and producing additional foliage. **4.** Pot-grown chrysanthemums. **5.** The life of annual climbers depends on the weather; remove foliage as soon as they die.

SPECIAL

SPECIAL

For fanatics/sun/summer: 1. Virginia creeper, *Parthenocissus* 'Veitchii', grown from a container. This self-clinging vine has small, green leaves which provide a perfect foil for summer flowers. The foliage turns vibrant orange-red in autumn. **2.** Hanging baskets suspended on brackets fixed to the timber façade are filled with petunias; lobelia; *Helichrysum*; ivy-leaved geraniums, *Pelargonium peltatum*; and fuchsias, which look effective viewed from underneath by someone sitting inside the room. **3.** Shallow balcony boxes contain the same arrangements as **2**, plus upright varieties of marigolds, *Calendula*; phlox; and tobacco plants, *Nicotiana*. **4.** Half-baskets or clay wall pots of summer trailing plants. Possibilities include: *Gazania; Achimenes; Nepeta;* and bellflowers, *Campanula isophylla*. **5.** The long box at the base of the balcony (maintained by ladder) follows the planting scheme for **3**.

Scented/sun: 1. Mimosa, *Acacia dealbata*, has pale grey-green foliage all year, and lemon-yellow scented flowers in early spring. **2.** *Viburnum carlesii* has very fragrant flowers in early summer; blush pink buds open to white. **3.** Summer jasmine, *Jasminum officinale*, is best in sunny aspects. It has perfumed white flowers. Trim it back hard in winter. *J. polyanthum* is an alternative variety for warmer climates. **4.** Window boxes contain *Skimmia* 'Rubella', which provides evergreen foliage and fragrant white flowers in late spring; large-flowered hyacinths for spring fragrance; and mignonette, *Reseda odorata*, for summer scent.

Overleaf: Trailing plants soften the elegant lines of the railings, while the brickwork provides a perfect foil for the background foliage.

WINTER

Evergreens come into their own during winter when their leaf colour, size and shape provide the basis for an effective display. Tumbling plants, especially ivies, break the harsh outlines of boxes or pots. Winter cherries over spring bulbs add splashes of colour.

Watering is vital. However, do not water in extremely cold weather, or if the boxes are adequately damp.

Sun: 1. The first flowers appear on the cherry's ▷ branches in mid-winter. Plant daffodils at the base of the tree if there is space. **2.** Ivy gives a green, softening effect all the year round. **3, 4.** As a contrast to the previous year, fill the boxes with pale pink hyacinths, 'Chestnut Flower' or 'Lady Derby', interplanted with forget-me-nots, *Myosotis*. **5.** Prune and train the vine as necessary, while it is dormant. **6.** Assess the permanent planting after removing the geraniums. Prune and/or put in new items before planting the bulbs. **7.** The clematis foliage remains green.

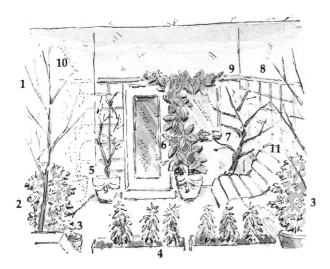

Shade: 1. The false acacias are dormant; prune if necessary. **2.** The hollies will berry quite well in a good season. **3.** The plantain lilies are dormant. **4.** Plant single, early, white tulips, 'Bellona', in groups between blocks of Siberian wallflowers, *Cheiranthus* x *allionii*. **5.** The clematis is dormant. **6.** The ivy provides a foliage edging around the window during winter. **7.** The sumac is a dormant sculptured framework. **8.** Trellis. **9.** Connecting rail. **10.** Mirrored wall. **11.** Seat.

Sun: 1. The candytuft maintains green stems throughout winter. **2.** Boxes. **3.** Winter cherries, *Solanum capsicastrum*, are grouped to provide accents in the centre and at the corners. Underplant them with narcissi 'Geranium'. **4.** Forget-me-nots, *Myosotis*. **5.** Grape hyacinths, *Muscari*, alternate with crocuses along the inside edges of the boxes so they can be viewed from the room.

△
For pets: 1. Put all boxes along the top of the balustrade, leaving the floor area free for washing down. Plant them with a range of evergreen and seasonal plants to suit aspect. (See 'Window Boxes' for suggestions.) Planting in continuous rows provides additional security for pets, and maximum visual effect. **2.** Heavy quality, plastic mesh cut to the height of the balustrade and wired to the back for fixing. **3.** Tap to facilitate watering the boxes and washing the floor. **4.** Container for climbing plants such as ivy, *Hedera.* Put it as high as possible from floor, out of reach of dogs and cats.

▽ This diagram shows how to construct a bracket to support a box on railings. **1.** Bracket. **2.** Capping. **3.** Vertical rails. **4.** Joining bar to prevent brackets from falling between the vertical rails; its width matches that of the capping overhang, to keep brackets vertical.

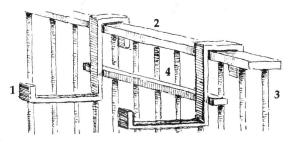

BACK GARDENS

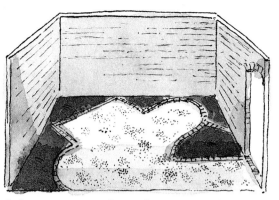

Soften a square garden and create attractive spaces with a curving ground plan.

STYLE & STRUCTURE

The design of back gardens, more than almost any other area, depends on personal preference. You may decide on perfect symmetry – or use a single object like an existing tree or a statue to create an asymmetrical layout. It may be necessary to set aside as much space as possible for entertaining or children's games. Alternatively, borders can be allowed to take over most of the plot.

A number of structural considerations must also be taken into account. If you want to extend an existing paved area, make sure it won't affect existing drainage patterns, or bridge the damp course on the house. Before raising border levels, check that the damp won't penetrate the walls of adjacent properties as a result.

There are three main guidelines to bear in mind if you decide to do some fairly radical reconstruction.

First, avoid small areas of lawn. They are time-consuming during summer, and often turn into muddy patches in winter.

Second, choose construction materials of the right scale, that blend with the environment: second-hand bricks and small paving stones for town gardens, local materials for country ones.

Finally, check your soil – and be prepared to spend time and money changing and improving it if necessary.

Circular beds echo the dining area and transform a conventional rectangular shape.

A tiny garden needs to grow upwards; train climbers on high walls and arches.

Left: Herbs and lettuces are mixed with pansies, shrubs and herbaceous perennials.

119

GREEN SKELETON

Sun

1. Broom, *Cytisus battandieri*, is trained to the wall with some branches allowed to come forward and thread through adjacent planting. It has silky, grey-green foliage, and yellow 'pineapple' flowers in early summer.
2. The spiralling foliage form of rosemary, *Rosmarinus officinalis*, enhances any border.
3. *Macleaya cordata* has bold foliage and coral flowers in summer; it emerges in spring to contrast with adjacent shrubs. **4.** *Ceanothus thyrsiflorus* 'Repens' has light blue flowers in late spring, and forms a mound across the corner, softening the raised border's edges.
5. The sun rose, *Cistus crispus*, has vivid cerise flowers carried continuously through summer and early autumn, and neat sage-green foliage. **6.** The strong leaf shapes of *Yucca filamentosa*, with spikes of cream flowers in mid-summer, contrast with: **7.** The rounded form of purple sage, *Salvia 'Purpurascens'*. **8.** Shrubs include *Cotoneaster dammeri* and *C. horizontalis*. The former holds its leaves throughout winter. **9.** The irises, *Iris stylosa*, have year-round foliage and bloom in winter. **10.** *Fremontia californica* has crinkled, green leaves. **11.** The grey-green, rose-tinted leaves of the fuchsia, *F.* 'Versicolor', are more important than the deep crimson flowers it bears in summer. **12.** Spaces for seasonal plantings.

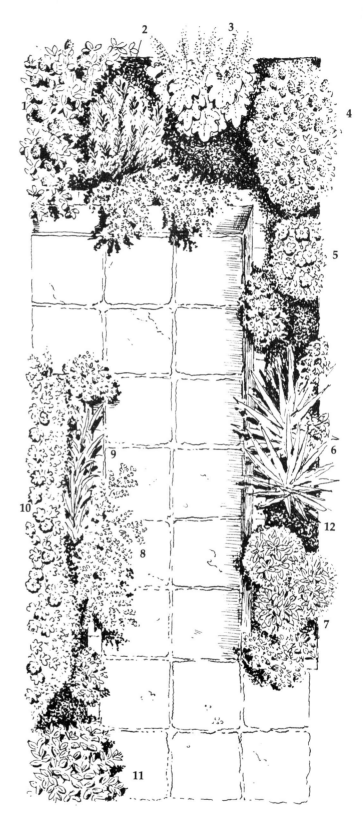

Sun

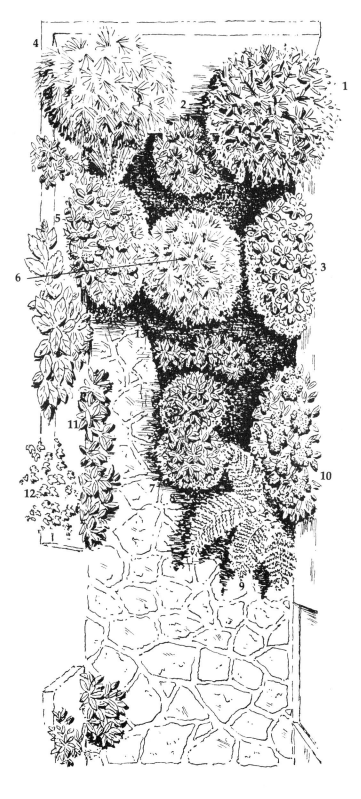

Shade

1. *Cotoneaster salicifolius*, a small standard tree, is evergreen with red berries in autumn. **2.** *Pieris* 'Forest Flame' has bright, young, red foliage. **3.** *Griselinia* is an attractive, easy-to-grow plant with bright, evergreen foliage. **4.** The bamboo, *Arundinaria murielae*, is softened at its base by: **5.** A group of *Viburnum davidii*; their dark green, leathery leaves are complemented by small, blue fruits in winter. **6.** The Japanese maple, *Acer palmatum* 'Dissectum Viridis', has space to stretch its horizontal branches with their finely cut, jade-green leaves. **7.** Evergreen azaleas, *A.* 'Palestrina', have white flowers in late spring. **8.** Bugle plant, *Ajuga reptans*, forms a ground cover for: **9.** The royal fern, *Osmunda regalis*. **10.** The hydrangea, *H. villosa*, has beautiful, hairy leaves, and lilac-blue, lace-cap flowers in mid-summer. **11.** Hellebore, *Helleborus corsicus*. **12.** Mix climbing plants like clematis, jasmine and honeysuckle to give year-round flowers; also ivy for abundant winter foliage. **13.** Spaces for seasonal plantings.

Shade

SPRING

Early narcissi, crocuses, daffodils and other bulbs are only some of the plants that come to life early in spring. Deciduous trees start to stir, while some shrubs bear spring flowers even before their leaves open: *Forsythia*, winter jasmine and the flowering quince are all examples. Camellias, marvellous as evergreens, have the added benefit of flowers that may open soon after midwinter in some situations.

In the middle of the season leaves unfold, and evergreen plants begin to show signs of growth. Late-flowering narcissi and tulips bloom, as do wallflowers, polyanthus and forget-me-nots. Herbaceous plants erupt from the ground, restoring interest to dull winter borders.

Late spring brings a great flush of rhododendrons and azaleas, their brilliantly coloured flowers offset by the fresh green leaves of adjacent plants – the climax of the gardening year for many people. The tiny garden, however, can only take one or two of these plants. Although they are magnificent in flower, their foliage is uninteresting for the rest of the year. Exceptions are the Japanese azaleas, which remain neat and tidy, and the small-flowered rhododendrons such as 'Blue TA'.

Other later flowering shrubs include varieties of viburnum (the marvellously scented *V. carlesii* is an example), shrubby brooms, and their sprawling counterparts like the cream-flowered *Cytisus kewensis*. *Kerria* has yellow, single or double flowers along its stems.

Spring is the season for pruning plants that will flower on wood during summer. Roses and some varieties of clematis are obvious examples.

Shade: 1. *Fatsia japonica* has large, distinctively shaped leaves. **2.** The plantain lilies, *Hosta*, and bear's breeches, *Acanthus spinosus*, are dormant. **3.** Small, single, early tulips. **4.** Hydrangea, *H. hortensia*; its leaves are just breaking. **5.** The new green and silver foliage of the ivy, *Hedera helix* 'Glacier', is about to emerge after winter. **6.** The apple or pear tree may be in blossom. **7.** The visual line of the circle under the tree is broken by naturalized early narcissi and crocuses, and shade-loving ground-cover plants such as cranesbill, *Geranium macrorrhizum*; or London pride, *Saxifraga umbrosa*. **8.** *Kerria japonica* has yellow flowers on leafless, bright green stems. The single-flowered variety is much prettier than the double variety, but does not retain its flowers as long. **9.** The camellia, C. x *williamsii* 'Donation', is in full flower, and trained to the wall. **10.** The dormant growth of the fuchsia, *F. magellanica* 'Riccartonii', should be pruned back quite heavily in early spring. **11.** The Japanese maple, *Acer palmatum* 'Dissectum Atropurpureum', is just breaking into bud. **12.** *Bergenia cordifolia* has large, leathery leaves and pink flowers in early spring. **13.** The variegated dogwood, *Cornus alba* 'Elegantissima', has bronze-red bark when dormant.

GARDEN PESTS

Aphids, also called greenfly, hatch in the warmth of early spring and, attracted to the new growth, can soon cover new shoots – especially in protected borders. Climbing plants, particularly roses and clematis, and the buds of late-opening tulips are especially at risk. Aphids pierce soft tissues and suck the sap, with the result that leaves are often mis-shaped when the shoots unfold.

To control aphids, spray plants lightly every seven to ten days – and continue to do so through-

Sun and shade: 1. False acacias, *Robinia pseudoacacia* 'Frisia', are dormant frameworks. **2.** The barberries *Berberis* x *stenophylla*, with their arching, evergreen stems, soften the bases of the false acacias and have yellow flowers. **3.** The Mexican mock oranges, *Choisya ternata*, have bright, evergreen foliage and white flowers which appear in mid-spring. **4.** *Hebe* 'Midsummer Beauty' has good, green foliage with reddish undersides to the leaves. **5.** *Viburnum* x *bodnantense* is a frost-resistant winter-flowering shrub. **6.** Pool with ivy, *Hedera helix* 'Jubilee' or *H. helix* 'Goldheart', on the wall behind it. **7.** Climbing plants include a grape vine, *Vitis vinifera* 'Purpurea'; a rose, 'Madame Alfred Carrière'; and clematis, *C.* x *jackmanii*. **8.** Climbing plants on the opposite wall include winter-flowering jasmine, *Jasminum nudiflorum*; a rose, *Rosa* 'Mermaid'; and clematis, *C.* x *henryi*. **9.** Species roses, *Rosa rubrifolia*, have violet stems. **10.** *Spiraea alpina*. **11.** *Perovskia*; prune plants back to their bases in early spring. **12.** Vases with seasonal plantings of forget-me-nots, *Myosotis*; and early, single tulips, 'Bellona'. **13.** Aubretia provides clumps of flowers among the paving stones.

Sun and shade: 1. Framework of passion flower, *Passiflora caerulea*. It may need pruning if frosts have cut back growth. **2.** The flowering crab apple, *Malus* 'Golden Hornet', is covered with white flowers on leafless branches. **3.** A selection of sun-loving shrubs at the base of the warm wall: *Santolina incana*; *Convolvulus cneorum*; and plumbago, *Ceratostigma willmottianum*. Plumbago must be cut back hard. **4.** *Mahonia japonica*; the racemes of yellow flowers are easily seen from the house. **5.** Mix *Skimmia* x *foremanii* and *S.* 'Rubella' to fertilize the spring flowers to produce autumn berries. **6.** The hellebore, *Helleborus corsicus*, has conspicuous creamy-green flowers in early spring. **7.** *Elaeagnus pungens* 'Maculata' produces bright green and gold foliage throughout the year. **8.** Lady's mantle, *Alchemilla mollis*, is dormant. **9.** The camellia, *C. japonica* 'Lady Vansittart', blooms in early spring; its flowers are white with a pale pink stripe. **10.** Bugle plants, *Ajuga reptans* 'Atropurpurea', are planted along the base of: **11.** A climbing hydrangea, *H. petiolaris*. **12.** The flowering quince, *Chaeonomeles speciosa* 'Pink Lady', flowers in early spring on leafless branches and makes a change from the usual crimson variety. **13.** Seasonal planting of bright pink, species tulips, 'Toronto'; late-flowering, double, white tulips, 'Mount Tacoma'; and narcissi 'February Gold'.

out summer – with one of the many different proprietary sprays on the market. Some contain lethal chemicals, others are also effective but less poisonous.

Another pest, active throughout summer, is a small, green caterpillar which attacks geraniums. Only a quarter-inch (5mm) long, it is difficult to spot. Tell-tale holes in leaves indicate its presence.

Like aphids, these caterpillars can be destroyed with proprietary sprays.

SUMMER

By early summer, rhododendrons and azaleas are past their best and will have been superseded by *Deutzia*, Mexican mock oranges and other shrubs. Clematis, honeysuckle and even roses begin to flower on the walls, although clematis, apart from some early-flowering varieties, will not produce its main effect until towards mid-summer. The same is true of most herbaceous plants although in many, like lady's mantle, attractive foliage is already adding variety to borders. All the silver foliage plants come into their own.

Put out bedding plants – half-hardy annuals and perennials – once all signs of frost have disappeared. If you can afford to buy full-grown geraniums, half-hardy fuchsias, etc., or had the patience to nurture them throughout winter, they will provide instant colour and continue to flower over a long period. In tiny gardens it is best to restrict these seasonal plantings to containers. If you do use them in borders, plant them informally and try to create small patches of colour to complement the surrounding foliage.

If you are establishing a new garden, remember that these half-hardy plants grow at a much faster pace than newly planted shrubs and may well swamp them unless you ensure that the latter have space to breathe.

In a good year summer can extend almost into autumn, with many shrubs continuing to provide flowers. *Ceratostigma* and *Caryopteris*, both with pale blue flowers, *Perovskia* with its lavender spires, and the hardy fuchsias are just a few such plants. Late-flowering climbing plants include *Hydrangea petiolaris* and the potato vines.

If your garden is sunny, try to find a spot for a few runner beans or tomato plants.

Continue spraying against pests and diseases. Greenfly multiply at a terrific rate and will destroy buds or cause the ensuing flowers to be malformed.

Summer is the time to enjoy your garden. Dabble by all means, spraying, weeding and removing dead flower heads, but, apart from remembering to water constantly, use summer as a time to sit back and relax.

Shade: 1. *Fatsia.* **2.** The plantain lilies and bear's breeches show full foliage patterns and contrasting leaves. **3.** Summer planting consists of busy Lizzie, *Impatiens*; and tobacco plants, *Nicotiana affinis.* **4.** Hydrangea. **5.** The ivy now bears its new blanket of young foliage. **6.** Apple or pear tree. **7.** Lilies of the valley, *Convallaria majalis*, take over from the narcissi and produce scented flowers in early summer. **8.** The *Kerria*, pruned immediately after flowering, produces light, interesting leaves for summer. **9.** Thoroughly mulch and feed the camellia after flowering. **10.** The fuchsia is covered with narrow, tubular, scarlet flowers from late summer onwards. **11.** The Japanese maple bears delicately carved, rich purple leaves. **12.** *Bergenia.* **13.** The dogwood has cream and green variegated leaves.

HINTS FOR DISABLED GARDENERS

Gardens with raised beds, or ones that make extensive use of taller vases, urns and other containers – balconies and roof gardens are obvious examples – are especially suitable for anyone who is disabled. (A specially designed planter is illustrated on page 157.) Easily reached window boxes, and hanging baskets that can be raised or lowered with pulleys, are also ideal for anyone who is handicapped.

Some adaptations may have to be made in a front or back garden, depending on the extent of the disability. Construct a ramp instead of steps for a wheelchair gardener, and limit borders to a maximum of 2ft (61cm) wide so that plants at the back can be easily reached. Paving stones must be very carefully laid – an uneven surface is hazardous for anyone. Use concrete with a finely corrugated

Sun and shade: 1. The false acacias have delicately formed, lime-green foliage. **2.** The barberries can be pruned after flowering to keep their shape. **3.** The Mexican mock oranges are covered in white, star-like flowers in early summer. **4.** The *Hebes* have pale lilac flowers throughout summer. **5.** Viburnum. **6.** Pool and ivy. **7.** The grape vine, rose and clematis are in flower. **8.** The rose and clematis are flowering on the opposite wall. **9.** The species roses have glaucous, purple foliage and clear pink flowers. **10.** The *Spiraea* are neat mounds covered with tiny, pink flowers. **11.** The *Perovskia* have grey-green foliage. **12.** Vases are planted with pink petunias, white geraniums (zonal pelargoniums) and grey *Helichrysum petiolatum*. **13.** Varieties of saxifrage and thyme flower among the paving stones.

Sun and shade: 1. The passion flower regains its foliage and produces its extraordinary flowers. **2.** Fruits are forming on the crab apple. **3.** Shrubs flower from early summer—*Santolina*—through to autumn—plumbago. **4.** Immediately after flowering, cut back any *Mahonia* branches which become too large. The plant will produce new, young clusters of foliage and look fresh and glossy throughout summer. **5.** *Skimmias*. **6.** The hellebore flowers gradually fade but the interesting foliage remains. **7.** New spring growth on the *Elaeagnus* gives more vivid colour in summer. **8.** The lady's mantle has attractive clumps of patterned foliage with stalks bearing dainty lemon-yellow flowers. **9.** Remove flowers from the camellia as they fade, and feed the plant. **10, 11:** Bugle plants and the hydrangea flower in June. **12.** Immediately after flowering, prune the quince and train it into shape. **13.** Vases contain seasonal plantings; select plants according to the aspect of each vase: petunias or ivy-leaved geraniums, *Pelargonium peltatum* for sun; fuchsias or busy Lizzie, *Impatiens*, for shade.

finish or rough-surfaced slabs that won't become slippery in bad weather; this advice, incidentally, applies to shady basements even when the gardener is able-bodied.

Choose self-supporting plants – geraniums, antirrhinums, petunias and many shrubs – that won't need tying and staking, and ground-covering plants like periwinkles, *Sedums*, ivies and alpine plants to reduce weeds and fall over the edges of raised containers.

Special tools for disabled people are available, or standard equipment can sometimes be adapted – an extra grip can be added to the handle of a conventional border fork, for example.

Finally, plastic pots, troughs and urns are all lighter – and less expensive – than clay or stone-ware versions.

Low maintenance/shade: 1. The sumac, *Rhus glabra* 'Laciniata', has fern-like, deeply incised leaves throughout summer, which turn orange, red and yellow in autumn. **2.** *Alchemilla alpina* produces small, green flowers. **3.** *Pachysandra terminalis* is a dwarf, evergreen sub-shrub. **4.** Sculpture. **5.** The winter sweet, *Chimonanthus praecox*, is fully leaved. **6.** The entire perimeter border is planted with Oregon grape, *Mahonia aquifolium*, which has good, evergreen foliage. It can be trimmed at any time, and should be kept back to reveal circular patterns where required. **7.** The new spikes of the elegant, narrow-leaved bamboo, *Arundinaria nitida*, are tall and arching. **8.** Dining area. (See page 132 for this garden in winter.)

Low maintenance/sun: 1. The flowering cherry, *Prunus* x *yedoensis*, flowers blush-white in late spring. **2.** Choose a rock rose, *Helianthemum*, in a colour that complements or contrasts with the cerise flowers of: **3.** The sun rose, *Cistus pulverulentus*; although its flowers open their petals in the morning and shed them in the afternoon, a good plant produces so many buds that it will flower richly for two or three months in a good summer. **4.** Sculpture. **5.** The corkscrew hazel, *Corylus* 'Contorta', keeps its attractive shape throughout summer. **6.** The grey mound of *Hebe albicans* acts as a foil to other colours. **7.** The lemon-yellow flowers of the bottle brush, *Callistemon salignus*, appear in early summer. **8.** The ivy, *Hedera helix* 'Sagittaefolia', has small, neat leaves and provides an easily kept, simple background to summer colours. **9.** Dining area. (See page 132 for this garden in winter.)

 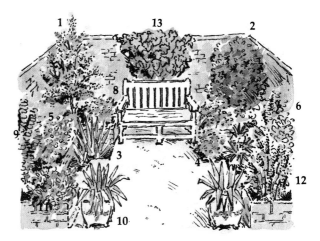

Foliage/shade: 1. The fig, *Ficus carica*, bears hand-some, lobed leaves. **2.** *Viburnum rhytidophyllum*, a leathery-leaved evergreen, carries creamy white flowers in early summer. **3.** The ivy, *Hedera arborescens*, is a shrubby form that creates a densely leaved mound. **4.** Solomon's seal, *Polygonatum* x *hybridum*, has white flowers on long stems; the whole plant presents an attractive, architectural form. **5.** *Rodgersia pinnata* has interesting foliage and pink flowers in summer. **6.** *Lonicera pileata* is a small-leaved semi-evergreen with a spreading habit. **7.** x *Fatshedera lizei* is a sprawling evergreen; its leaf shape is between ivy and *Fatsia*. **8.** A low-growing yew, *Taxus repandians*. **9.** *Fatsia japonica* 'Variegata'; its large, palmate leaves, tipped with cream, give a sub-tropical effect. **10.** Vases containing half-hardy ferns: *Nephrolepsis* is easily available from florists and garden centres. **11.** Plantain lilies, *Hosta fortunei* 'Albopicta', have striking, broad-bladed leaves, cream with green margins. **12.** *Aralia elata* 'Variegata' is dramatic in summer, with huge leaves in green and cream variegations. **13.** A very large-leaved ivy, *Hedera colchica*, is trained as a climber. (See page 133 for this garden in winter.)

Foliage/sun: 1. The sea buckthorn, *Hippophae rham-noides*, has narrow, silvery leaves. **2.** The deep, wine-purple leaves of the smokebush, *Cotinus coggygria* 'Foliis Purpureis', redden in autumn. **3.** Flax, *Phormium tenax*, comes in many variegated forms and recently introduced varieties. *P.t.* 'Purpureum' has bronze-purple foliage, and *P.t.* 'Variegatum' has leaves striped with green and yellow. **4.** *Senecio greyi* has new, silver foliage and produces yellow flowers in summer. **5.** Jerusalem sage, *Phlomis fruticosa*, is a shrubby evergreen with yellow flowers and grey-green leaves. **6.** *Griselina littoralis*. **7.** *Chamaerops humilis* has fan-shaped, palm-like leaves. **8.** *Hebe* 'Subalpina' produces white flowers in mid-summer. **9.** The new, silver foliage of the gum tree, *Eucalyptus gunnii*, is particularly attractive. **10.** Vases are planted with cabbage palm, *Cordyline indivisa*; it holds its form throughout the year. **11.** Fuchsias, *F.* 'Versicolor', have branches of silver, grey-green leaves tipped with pink. **12.** The attractive, pink-tinged foliage of the sacred bamboo, *Nandina domestica*, will turn vivid orange in autumn. **13.** The large, green leaves of the splendidly ornamental glory vine, *Vitis coignetiae*, have mist-coloured undersides and will turn copper, orange and yellow in autumn. (See page 133 for this garden in winter.)

AUTUMN

There are three main areas of interest in autumn gardens.

The first is the colour provided by flowers. The climbing rose 'Mermaid', for example, continues to bloom well into autumn, as do some herbaceous plants like asters and the showy *Sedum spectabile*. The remnants of summer bedding plants – geraniums, dahlias, begonias and busy Lizzie – contribute colour, as do late-flowering shrubs like hydrangeas and *Ceratostigma*.

The second is the autumn shades that appear as evenings become cooler and the foliage on many plants begins to die. Japanese maples, sumacs and *Cotinus* come into this second group. Flowering cherries, deciduous azaleas and peonies also have colourful leaves, in addition to their earlier flowers.

The third area is fruit and berries. Although small gardens provide limited scope for fruit trees, berried plants abound. Firethorns and varieties of *Cotoneaster* are the best known. Remember that berries, like other fruits, only appear once a plant has flowered and that they therefore do best in conditions that encourage flowering: sunshine or good light.

Autumn-flowering crocuses, *Colchicum*, add interest at this time of the year. They are larger and taller than conventional crocuses, and their pale mauve, leafless spikes emerge in fresh contrast to the mellowness of surrounding plants.

There are few chores. Remove fallen leaves covering lawns and low or soft plants, and seasonal plants damaged by frost.

Shade: 1. The *Fatsia* has white, lantern flowers in mid-autumn. **2.** The plantain lilies and bear's breeches flower at the end of summer. **3.** Remove summer planting when it is killed by frost. Plant wallflowers, *Cheiranthus* x *allionii*, and tall tulips, 'Darwin' or 'Triumph'. **4.** The hydrangea is in flower. **5.** Ivy. **6.** Harvest fruit from the tree. **7.** The leaves of lilies of the valley turn yellow. **8.** *Kerria*. **9.** Camellia. **10.** The fuchsia continues to flower. **11.** The leaves of the Japanese maple turn brown and orange. **12.** The *Bergenia* looks particularly good with the new leaves it has produced in the course of summer. **13.** The leaves of the dogwood turn yellow.

PRUNING

There are three main reasons for pruning plants: to keep them tidy; to encourage them to grow in a particular shape; and to channel their energies into producing flowers or fruit.

Although details of timing, severity, etc vary according to the plant, the basic technique is simple. All you have to do is make a cut about ⅛in. (3mm) above a bud from which a new stem will grow. The cut must slope gently downwards from the bud which should face the direction in which you want the new shoot to grow. Use a very sharp knife or pruning shears, or a pruning saw for small trees or large shrubs.

Trees, shrubs and climbers
Trees and shrubs generally need to be pruned more often in small gardens in order to contain their size – but only prune if absolutely necessary.

Prune plants that flower on the previous season's growth after flowering, removing weak and untidy growth and most of the flowering spikes, and

Sun and shade: 1. The leaves of the false acacias turn golden yellow. **2.** Barberries. **3.** Mexican mock oranges. **4.** The *Hebes* continue to flower into autumn. **5.** Viburnums bear sweetly scented, rose-tinted flowers in late autumn. **6.** Pool and ivy. **7.** The leaves of the grape vine take on a brighter colour. **8.** The rose continues to flower well into autumn. Tie in and prune back in late autumn or early winter. **9.** Rose hips begin to colour. **10.** *Spiraea* continues to flower. **11.** Tall sprays of lavender-blue flowers appear on the *Perovskia*. **12.** Geraniums flower into autumn.

Sun and shade: 1. The passion flower continues until frosts curtail flowering. **2.** The crab apple has bright yellow fruit. **3.** The shrubs have grown and the plumbago is still flowering. **4.** *Mahonia.* **5.** Berries appear on the *Skimmias*. **6.** Trim the foliage of the hellebore and generally tidy the plant ready for winter. **7.** *Elaeagnus.* **8.** Remove the leaves from the lady's mantle as it goes into its dormant state. **9.** Camellia. **10, 11:** Leaves turn on the bugle plants and hydrangea as winter approaches. **12.** Flowering quince. **13.** Vases carry their flowers well into autumn; individual vases may be replenished with chrysanthemums or other bright, berried plants.

cutting them to shape. If it is necessary to thin the plant, remove one or two shoots from just above ground level.

Plants that flower from stems formed during the same season are pruned in late winter or early spring before growth starts. They can often be severely cut back – to ground level if new stems or foliage are the major attraction of the plant.

Always ask your supplier for technical advice on when plants should be pruned, etc. Aesthetic decisions will be up to you.

Pruning rules are basically the same for climbing plants, although vigorous specimens like passion flower occasionally require drastic treatment to prevent untidy growth.

Roses

Prune roses to discourage crossing stems and to prevent dense growth in the centre of the plant. Always make cuts at outward-facing buds, and make it a rule to remove as much stem when you are deadheading as you would if you were picking flowers for a vase. This will encourage new growth and a second flush of flowers.

Pruning climbing roses is an important autumn task. After flowering, the plant produces strong shoots, some of which may be 5ft or 6ft (about 1½m to 2m) long by early autumn; others will be shorter and weaker. Arch the sturdiest shoots over and tie the tips into supporting wires or trellis work, almost level with where they emerge from the main stem. If shoots are thrown up from the base, use them to fill in lower areas. Reduce the weaker shoots, and those which have already borne clusters of roses, to short spurs about 4in. (10cm) long.

Do this every year and you will gradually build up a framework that covers the fence or wall behind the plant. The spurs will ensure an abundant crop of flowers.

WINTER

The true test of design is whether a garden remains interesting and attractive during winter. Evergreens are the key to success. They hold their form and help to retain balance in plant groupings, and some even produce flowers. *Mahonia*, for example, bears sweetly scented blooms during the bleak days of late winter. Evergreen climbers are essential on walls – the variegated forms of ivy are cheerful throughout winter.

Winter-flowering deciduous shrubs add an extra dimension with short flowering spells. Colours are generally pale and subtle, but prized nevertheless during grey months when they bring life to an otherwise dormant world. The 'Rosea' form of the autumn-flowering cherry, a favourite tree in small gardens, bears pink flowers through to early spring.

Deciduous shrubs like sumacs and contorted hazels have interesting shapes. Carefully positioned, they will break the hard line of a fence or create a striking silhouette against a blank wall or the winter sky.

The tracery of many self-clinging wall plants has its own beauty, particularly on pale brickwork, while the silken seed-heads of some varieties of clematis are truly delightful.

Vases and sculpture also add interest. Plant containers with winter cherries, polyanthus or winter pansies to create patches of colour against paved areas or the main outlines of borders.

Blue irises, *Iris stylosa*, can appear as early as mid-winter, and *Bergenia* with its leathery leaves bears pink flowers at about the same time. Finally there are the narcissi. Although technically they flower in winter, most people regard them as the first heralds of spring.

Bulbs should be planted by early winter. At the same time take the opportunity to cultivate small open spaces, lifting out spent summer plantings and lightly pruning shrubs that have gone out of control. The only other task at this time is to remove dead leaves from borders.

Prune deciduous shrubs and climbing plants (with the exception of roses) after mid-winter. This applies particularly to vines, which must only be cut when they are completely dormant.

Shade: 1. *Fatsia*; in a mild year, the strong, evergreen foliage carries flowers right into winter. **2.** The plantain lilies and bear's breeches are dormant. **3.** The wallflowers provide some greenery and will combine with the tall tulips to make a spring display. **4.** The hydrangea loses its leaves but holds its dried brown flowers; do not remove these until the end of winter. **5.** The ivy's winter foliage is effective. **6.** Apple or pear tree. **7.** The narcissi re-emerge. **8.** Green stems on the *Kerria* provide interest even without flowers or leaves. **9.** In a protected garden the first flowers on the camellia may appear in early winter. **10.** Fuschia. **11.** Japanese maple. **12.** The *Bergenia* often produces its first flowers in mid-winter. **13.** Prune the dogwood to encourage new wood and keep the tree under control in this confined space.

Sun and shade: 1. False acacias. **2.** Barberries. **3.** Mexican mock oranges. **4.** *Hebes*. **5.** Viburnum. **6.** Pool and ivy. **7.** Climbing plants. **8.** The rose can carry its leaves nearly to mid-winter. Jasmine is in flower. **9.** Colourful rose hips last into early winter. **10.** *Spiraea*. **11.** *Perovskia*. **12.** Winter cherry, *Solanum capsicastrum*, with narcissi packed underneath. The *Helichrysum* can remain as silver foliage until it is totally destroyed by frost.

Sun and shade: 1. The passion flower probably needs light trimming to look neat through winter. **2.** The leafless crab apple still carries fruit. **3.** Shrubs are trimmed as necessary to maintain their shapes. **4.** The earliest flowers of the *Mahonia* appear in mid-winter. **5.** The *Skimmias* provide form and shape, with the added attraction of berries, throughout winter. **6.** The hellebore starts flowering in late winter. **7.** The *Elaeagnus* remains bright and attractive. **8.** The lady's mantle is dormant. **9.** The camellia may begin flowering in mid-winter in really protected areas. **10.** The bugle plants retain their foliage. **11.** The hydrangea can be trimmed to prevent branches from obstructing doorways or window openings. **12.** Flowering quince. **13.** Vases are planted for spring displays. Combine tulips and wallflowers, *Cheiranthus*, or simply fill the containers with narcissi or short, multi-headed tulips.

DAFFODILS

Although most people regard daffodils, those golden-yellow harbingers of spring, as being in a class of their own, they are in fact part of the genus *Narcissus*. Also known as trumpet narcissi, they are distinguished from the plants commonly known as narcissi by the fact that their central trumpet is always as long as, or longer than, the surrounding petals.

Daffodils fall into three of the 11 divisions into which garden varieties of the genus *Narcissus* are separated, and come in various colour combinations as well as yellow: cream or white petals with yellow trumpets, for example, or all-white flowers.

Traditional, 'all-yellow' daffodils include 'Dutch Master', 'Golden Harvest' and 'Golden Rapture' as well as 'Van Sion' (the common, early, double daffodil), 'Cheerfulness' and 'Thalia'.

Confusingly, several varieties of garden narcissi are also all-yellow: 'Carlton', 'February Gold', 'Peeping Tom' and 'Galway' are just a few examples.

Winter continued

Low maintenance/shade: 1. The dormant sumac has a sculptural shape which remains attractive throughout winter. **2.** The *Alchemilla* is a grey-green, silvery foliage carpet during early winter. **3.** The *Pachysandra* has spikes of greenish-white flowers in late winter. **4.** Sculpture. **5.** The winter sweet has pale yellow, waxen flowers on bare stems in mid-winter. Cut back to the required size immediately after flowering. **6.** The Oregon grape has yellow flowers in early spring. **7.** Bamboo. **8.** Dining area. (See page 126 for this garden in summer.)

Low maintenance/sun: 1. The graceful, arching branches of the flowering cherry are attractive even in winter. **2.** The rock rose has fine, spreading, grey-green foliage. **3.** The sun rose has sage-green leaves and is the neatest and most architectural plant in its family. **4.** Sculpture. **5.** The curiously contorted branches of the corkscrew hazel bear catkins in winter. **6.** The *Hebe* makes a neat mound of grey foliage. **7.** The bottle brush, with its loose, evergreen form, is only suitable for milder climates. **8.** Dining area. (See page 126 for this garden in summer.)

SEASONAL COLOUR

Seasonal plantings provide temporary but vivid splashes of colour. This list highlights some of the suggestions in this book.

Spring: Crocuses; forget-me-nots, *Myosotis;* grape hyacinths, *Muscari;* hyacinths; narcissi; polyanthus, *Primula polyantha; Scilla sibirica;* tulips; wallflowers, *Cheiranthus.*

Summer: *Achimenes;* alyssum; begonias; busy Lizzie, *Impatiens; Calceolaria;* cineraria; flame nettles, *Coleus;* French marigolds, *Tagetes patula;* fuchsias; *Gazania;* geraniums (zonal pelargoniums); ivy-leaved geraniums, *Pelargonium peltatum;* lobelias; marigolds, *Tagetes;* mesembryanthemums; pansies, *Viola* x *wittrockiana;* salvia; bellflowers, *Campanula isophylla;* tobacco plants, *Nicotiana.*

Autumn: Chrysanthemums; dahlias.

Winter: Cape heather, *Erica gracilis;* ornamental peppers, *Capsicum frutescens;* winter-flowering cherries, *Solanum capsicastrum.*

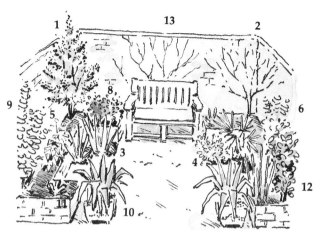

Foliage/shade: 1. The fig makes an interestingly shaped framework, even when dormant. **2.** Viburnum. **3.** Ivy. **4.** Solomon's seal is dormant. **5.** The *Rodgersia* is also dormant. **6.** *Lonicera.* **7.** *Fatshedera.* **8.** Yew. **9.** *Fatsia japonica.* **10.** Vases planted with spotted laurel, *Aucuba crotonifolia.* **11.** The plantain lilies are dormant. **12.** The *Aralia* is a dormant stem. **13.** Large-leaved ivy. (See page 127 for this garden in summer.)

Foliage/sun: 1. The sea buckthorn bears orange berries in autumn and winter. **2.** The smokebush is dormant. Prune it into shape to keep it in bounds. **3.** Flax. **4.** The *Senecio* has grey-green leaves and a tumbling habit. **5.** Jerusalem sage. **6.** The *Griselina* keeps its bright green foliage throughout winter. **7.** *Chamaerops.* **8.** The tiny leaves of the *Hebe* form a ball of bright green foliage. **9.** Prune the gum tree at the beginning of spring to ensure new silver growth. **10.** Vases planted with cabbage palms. **11.** The fuchsias, now dormant, should be pruned near to base in early spring. **12.** The sacred bamboo is a clump of dormant stems. **13.** The glory vine is a brown framework on the wall. (See page 127 for this garden in summer.)

ALKALINE AND ACID SOILS

Degrees of acidity and alkalinity in soil are measured on a 'PH' scale with a neutral point of 7. Readings below this indicate acidity, ones above mean an increase in alkalinity. Meters and analytical testing kits are available from garden shops – and essential if you are starting a new garden.

Acid-loving plants, often known as erinaceous plants, include azaleas and rhododendrons. Dogwoods, viburnums and clematis are among the plants that will thrive in an alkaline soil.

A neutral soil will grow a wide range of plants, but even so you will need to help erinaceous varieties along. Free lime locks up the iron in the soil preventing the latter's absorption by the plant and resulting in a yellowing of the leaves. The remedy is to add an iron chelate compound to the soil, in quantities specified by the manufacturer.

Alkaline-loving plants will benefit if lime is included when the soil is prepared.

Cottage garden: The essence of a cottage garden is informality and individual expression. At its best in summer, it changes constantly as a wide range of mainly herbaceous plants flower and fade. Although it can seem rather dull in winter, it can be brightened up with traditional, early-flowering shrubs. **1.** Low-growing plants, such as bellflowers, *Campanula garganica; Aubretia;* thyme, *Thymus vulgaris;* and the primulas *P.* 'Wanda' and *P. auricula*, fill cracks between informally laid paving stones. **2.** Shrubs provide winter form while maintaining the 'feel' of the garden. Lavender, *Lavandula;* a single-flowered *Kerria;* and rosemary, *Rosmarinus officinalis*, are all appropriate. **3.** The summer-flowering rose 'Albertine' is intertwined with clematis, *C.* x 'Lasurstern'. Another lovely, summer-flowering climber is the honeysuckle, *Lonicera periclymenum*, in its early- and late-flowering forms. **4.** Early spring-flowering wall shrubs and climbers such as Japanese quince, *Chaenomeles japonica*, and winter jasmine, *J. nudiflorum*. **5.** Summer herbaceous plants can include: hollyhocks, *Althaea rosea; Nepeta;* cranesbill, *Geranium;* and anemones, *A. japonica*.

Useful: 1. Green beans, *Phaseolus coccineus*. **2.** A fan-trained peach, *Prunus persica*, against the wall. **3.** Fan-trained Morello cherry, *Prunus cerasus* 'Morello'. **4.** Soft fruit can include gooseberries, *Ribes grossularia*. **5.** Blackberries, *Rubus fruticosus;* and loganberries, *R.* x *loganobaccus*. **6.** Sweet bays, *Laurus nobilis*. **7.** Strawberry pot. **8.** Herbs, held to pattern, include chervil, *Anthriscus cerefolium;* parsley, *Petroselinum crispum;* thyme, *Thymus;* basil, *Ocimum basilicum;* and chives, *Allium schoenoprasum*. **9.** Crop area for tomatoes, lettuces and other salad vegetables.

Left: An ingenious use of space; this water garden even has stepping stones across the pool.

Glass-covered/shade: 1. Mirror with fountain mask. **2.** Mirror in alcove. **3.** Panels of diamond mesh trellis in alcoves and on sides of raised beds and pool. **4.** Corner groupings of plants: a camellia, *C. japonica* 'Adolphe Audusson'; a *Fatsia*; hardy ferns, *Asplenium* and *Pteridium*; and perhaps an aspidistra. **5.** A handsome Norfolk Island pine, *Araucaria excelsa*. **6.** Glass roof. **7.** Hanging baskets contain ferns and half-hardy trailing fuchsias.

Scented/evening sun/summer: 1. *Buddleia* 'Lochinch' has greyish, young leaves and dark purple flowers. **2.** White, double lilac *Syringa* 'Madame Lemoine'. **3.** Mexican mock orange, *Choisya ternata*. **4.** *Daphne odora* has clear pink flowers in early spring. **5.** The mock orange, *Philadelphus* 'Manteau d'Hermine', produces creamy white, double flowers in summer. **6.** Hybrid tea rose 'Fragrant Cloud'. **7.** *Viburnum carlesii* has pale blush flowers on leafless stems in mid-spring. **8.** Witch hazel, *Hamamelis mollis*, has yellow flowers on leafless branches from winter to early spring. **9.** The shrubby honeysuckle, *Lonicera fragrantissima*, is partially ever-green and bears small, white flowers all through winter. **10.** The broom, *Cytisus x praecox*, has rich cream flowers during late spring and early summer. **11.** Climbing plants include jasmine, *Jasminum officinale*, and honeysuckle, *Lonicera periclymenum* 'Serotina'. **12.** *Skimmia* and Christmas box, *Sarcococca humilis*, hold up well in shade. **13.** Containers are filled with single, white geraniums to make an evening show. **14.** Borders are planted with night-scented stocks, *Matthiola bicornis*, and tobacco plants, *Nicotiana affinis*. **15.** Lilies; *Lilium auratum* is heavily scented.

Glass-covered/sun: 1. Seat. **2.** Terracotta pot with calamondin orange, *Citrus mitis*. **3.** Raised beds with mimosa, *Acacia dealbata*; bottle brush, *Callistemon salignus*; *Leptospermum scoparium*; and scented-leaf geraniums, *Pelargonium tomentosum*. **4.** Basket of ivy-leaved geraniums, *Pelargonium* 'L'Elégante'. **5.** Blue plumbago, *P. capensis*; jasmine, *Jasminum polyanthum*; and two plants treated as annuals: morning glory, *Ipomoea tricolor*, and *Cobaea scandens*. **6.** Pots planted with Kafir lilies, *Clivia miniata* and African lilies, *Agapanthus africanus*.

Tiny/shade: 1. Wall mask fountain with arched surround. **2.** The ivy, *Hedera helix* 'Goldheart', has small, gold and green leaves. **3.** A low Japanese maple, *Acer palmatum* 'Dissectum', is backed by arching sprays of bamboo, *Arundinaria murielae*. **4.** Summer planting of busy Lizzie, *Impatiens*, and tobacco plants, *Nicotiana affinis*. **5.** *Osmanthus delavayi*, an evergreen flowering shrub, has neat, green foliage and tiny, highly perfumed white flowers in mid-spring. **6.** Barrenwort, *Epimedium grandiflorum*, is a good foliage plant with pale yellow flowers in spring. **7.** The golden hop, *Humulus lupulus* 'Aureus', scrambles on mesh set against the wall. It has bright lime-yellow foliage throughout summer and dies back in winter. **8.** A mirrored arch with ivy, *Hedera* 'Cristata', trained along the sides.

Tiny/sun: 1. Wall mask fountain. **2.** Clematis, C. *macropetala*, has small, dull blue, double flowers in early summer, followed by silken seed heads. **3.** The variegated bamboo, *Arundinaria variegata*, is combined with an upright-growing Japanese maple, *Acer palmatum*. **4.** Summer planting of geraniums (zonal pelargoniums) in colours you prefer. **5.** *Senecio* 'White Diamond' has striking, silver foliage. **6.** A low carpet of bellflowers, *Campanula poscharskyana*, with blue star-like flowers through summer to late autumn. **7.** A climbing flowering maple, *Abutilon megapotamicum*. The shrub produces yellow and red flowers throughout summer and must be pinned back against the wall. **8.** A mirrored centre archway with wisteria, *Wistaria sinensis*, trained over the trellis so that the flowers hang in front of the mirror in spring.

For children: 1. Paving stones alternate with strips of artificial grass under play equipment. **2.** Heavy beams, fixed on the house walls with joist hangers, support a variety of play equipment: **3.** Swings. **4.** Rope ladder. **5.** Netball ring. The beams also support climbing plants. **6.** The tall trellis helps to contain balls. **7.** The narrow perimeter border, filled entirely with climbing plants, softens walls and trellis. Avoid plants which might puncture balls. Suggestions for sun include: jasmine, *Jasminum officinale*; clematis, C. *montana*, and C. *armandii*; and vines, *Vitis vinifera* 'Purpurea' and V. *coignetiae*. Possibilities for shade are: jasmine, *Jasminum nudiflorum*; clematis, C. x *jackmanii*; Virginia creeper, *Parthenocissus henryana*; and the climbing rose 'Zéphirine Drouhin'.

Overleaf: A shady corner in early summer; the blend of fresh green foliage contrasts with the warmth of an old, clay chimney pot.

ROOF GARDENS

Contemporary roof garden; strategically placed evergreen shrubs ensure year-round interest.

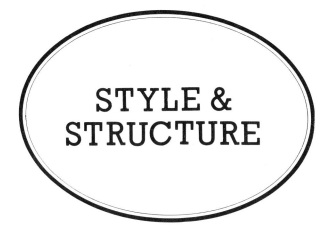

STYLE & STRUCTURE

Roof gardens, like balconies and basements, can be treated as extensions of the interior, with the style of the room reflected in furniture and containers. Remember too that the garden should be designed to be attractive and interesting all year round, in winter as well as summer.

Roofs are designed to accept certain loadings. The norm for a concrete slab is 30lb to 40lb per square foot (about 13.5kg to 18kg per 0.09 square metres). In round terms this means you can allow approximately 12 inches (about 30 centimetres) of

Three roof-garden sites. **1.** The wind will affect tall plants at this level. **2.** A more sheltered garden, but still keep plantings low. **3.** Walls give protection against the wind.

reasonably moist soil, providing you choose or build lightweight containers. This depth can be increased slightly if you stand heavier boxes and tubs in corners or at sides where the concrete is adequately supported by the adjacent wall.

Roofs constructed of wood and finished in lead or a lightweight material with a bituminous surface support less weight – 20lb to 30lb per square foot (about 9kg to 13.5kg per 0.09 square metres) is the limit. Establish where the joists of wooden roofs run into the walls. Once again the areas immediately adjacent to the walls will be the strongest parts.

It is essential to consult a surveyor if you are in any doubt at all about the structural make-up of your roof or its strength. If you suspect any leaks, have these checked and sealed by a professional before starting to create your garden.

Any major alteration to the skyline – extending existing railings or making a pergola or covered area – generally requires official permission. Always check before spending time and money on structural changes.

Trellis work and other screening materials must be firmly secured or they may fall and injure people below. Winds can be much stronger on roof tops than at ground level, and wind resistance is increased when an open screen is covered with plants – with a greater risk of its being blown over. Another problem is that taller plants can be distorted by the wind.

Soft materials like asphalt, bitumen, etc. must be protected from the sharp lower edges of containers, furniture and pointed heels. Ceramic tiles are a sensible choice for a durable surface. Paving stones can be used, but you will obviously have to subtract their weight from an already slender allowance. Tiles and paving stones should be laid by a professional. Or you could construct a 'deck' from wooden planks or duckboard – and use the same pattern to face inexpensive containers.

Finally, increased wind speeds at roof-top level dry out compost more quickly than in other areas; roof gardens are subject almost to drought conditions. A good, easily operated water supply – preferably a tap on the roof – is essential for success.

GREEN SKELETON

Sun

1. Clematis, *C. armandii*; white flowers highlight its evergreen leaves in spring. **2.** The golden hop, *Humulus lupulus* 'Aureus' forms a tangle of golden foliage. **3.** The mimosa, *Acacia dealbata*, has fern-like, grey-green

Sun

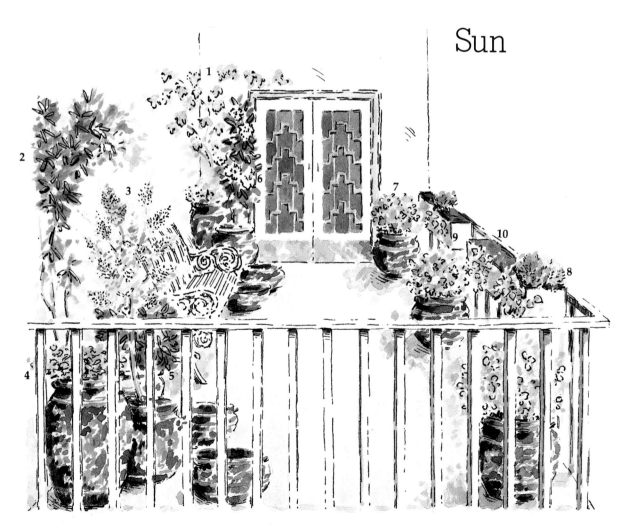

foliage. **4.** *Ballota pseudo-dictamnus* is a distinctive, round-leaved, foliage plant. **5.** The dark green bay, *Laurus nobilis*, is trained into a bush shape. **6.** Plenty of water is needed to keep the polished, evergreen foliage of the summer-flowering *Magnolia grandiflora* at its best. **7.** *Pittosporum tenuifolium* 'Garnettii' has variegated foliage and a rounded yet informal habit. **8.** *Hebe albicans* forms dense mounds of blue-grey foliage. **9.** The grey, tumbling foliage of *Helichrysum petiolatum* survives until winter. **10.** Spaces in wall-hung boxes and containers for seasonal plantings.

Shade

1. The green foliage and small leaves of *Hedera helix* 'Chicago' withstand the wind. **2.** *H. helix* 'Glacier' has neat, variegated foliage. **3.** The firethorns, *Pyracantha* 'Orange Glow', are among the best shrubs for cold, wintry, roof conditions. **4.** The yews, *Taxus* 'Repens', have dark, evergreen foliage. **5.** The maidenhair tree, *Ginkgo biloba* provides a vertical accent. **6.** *Mahonia aquifolium*. **7.** Fill pots with honey locust, *Gleditsia triacanthos* 'Sunburst'; prune back each spring to restrict growth. **8.** Boxes hung on the rail are filled with tough, evergreen *Euonymus fortunei*. The plants cover the boxes, tumbling over the sides. **9.** Paint the wall pale terracotta. **10.** The ornamental seat doubles as 'sculpture' in winter. **11.** Seasonal plantings.

In both these designs taller plants are against walls where they are less prone to wind damage.

Shade

SPRING

Anyone who has a roof garden will want to use it for the longest possible period during the year. Although the sun is often warm enough for enjoyable gardening – or even sitting out – by mid- or late spring, the wind can cancel out this warmth unless the area is properly protected by some kind of screening. In some gardens it may be logical to screen the entire perimeter of the roof; in others, the only solution may be to construct a sheltered seating area.

Provided that some protection is given to planting areas, the first narcissi will be in bloom by early spring – or even late in winter. Short-stemmed and small-headed, they are able to withstand the wind that bedevils most roof gardens. Bulbs are normally restricted to vases, or planted as clusters among other plants.

Similarly, other spring plants like polyanthus, wallflowers and forget-me-nots are best tucked into the framework of established shrubs, which provide foliage contrast and, in the case of camellias, some flowers.

Herbs are generally available from retailers or growers from early to mid-spring, and pots planted entirely with parsley, thyme, chives or tarragon provide an immediate source of flavourings for the kitchen. Remember, though, that sweet basil can only be put out when all frosts have passed. Herbs like rosemary and rue are major foliage plants once established, while thyme makes an attractive edging.

Careful watering is essential to make sure that beds and containers don't dry out. This is especially important in mid-spring when winds are still cold and drying – and potentially disastrous to newly planted shrubs. Many plants are expected to achieve considerable size – climbers, for example, are required to cover blank walls or perimeter trellis work – even though their root development is restricted by containers or small beds. An unrestricted supply of water is essential, and if this is not provided during early spring they will fail to put on growth.

Shade: 1. The clematis, *C.* 'Nelly Moser', is a tracery of old wood with occasional seed heads. A hardy fuchsia, *F.* 'Tom Thumb' is planted at its base. **2.** *Pyracantha rogersiana* is underplanted with: **3.** The bright, evergreen spotted laurel, *Aucuba crotonifolia.* **4.** Two containers are given over to seasonal plantings of forget-me-nots, *Myosotis*; violas; and pale cream narcissi. **5.** Japanese maples, *Acer palmatum* 'Dissectum viridis', weep over the front edges of the centre vases. Behind the maples, *Skimmia fortunei* provides winter foliage and early spring flowers. **6.** The ivy, *Hedera helix* 'Chicago', planted at the rear of the pots is tough enough to tumble over the railings. **7.** Closely woven nylon mesh, stretched across the railings, gives protection from the wind. **8.** The camellia, *C.* x *williamsii* 'J. C. Williams', climbs into the corner; its bright pink flowers show from early spring. **9.** The seat is untreated hardwood, allowed to silver, and brightened with pale green cushions when in use.

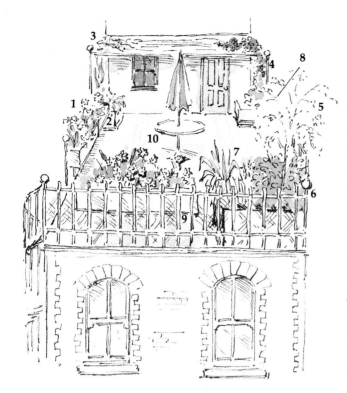

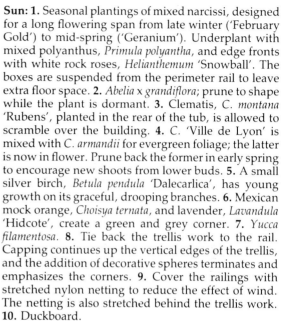

Sun: 1. Seasonal plantings of mixed narcissi, designed for a long flowering span from late winter ('February Gold') to mid-spring ('Geranium'). Underplant with mixed polyanthus, *Primula polyantha*, and edge fronts with white rock roses, *Helianthemum* 'Snowball'. The boxes are suspended from the perimeter rail to leave extra floor space. **2.** *Abelia* x *grandiflora*; prune to shape while the plant is dormant. **3.** Clematis, *C. montana* 'Rubens', planted in the rear of the tub, is allowed to scramble over the building. **4.** *C.* 'Ville de Lyon' is mixed with *C. armandii* for evergreen foliage; the latter is now in flower. Prune back the former in early spring to encourage new shoots from lower buds. **5.** A small silver birch, *Betula pendula* 'Dalecarlica', has young growth on its graceful, drooping branches. **6.** Mexican mock orange, *Choisya ternata*, and lavender, *Lavandula* 'Hidcote', create a green and grey corner. **7.** *Yucca filamentosa*. **8.** Tie back the trellis work to the rail. Capping continues up the vertical edges of the trellis, and the addition of decorative spheres terminates and emphasizes the corners. **9.** Cover the railings with stretched nylon netting to reduce the effect of wind. The netting is also stretched behind the trellis work. **10.** Duckboard.

Formal: 1. Surface of artificial grass. **2.** Mop-headed bay trees, *Laurus nobilis*, in ornamental wooden tubs (*caisses Versailles*). **3.** Box, *Buxus*, in low boxes lightly ornamented to match the tubs. **4.** Bay, *L. nobilis*, pruned to form blocks. **5.** A central 'classic' vase in fibreglass or terracotta depending on the weight your roof can sustain. Fill it with flowers and foliage for summer colour: pink, ivy-leaved geraniums, *Pelargonium peltatum* 'Galilee', or red geraniums *P.* 'Paul Crampel' (zonal). Alternatively, combine white, single geraniums (zonal pelargoniums) with lime-green flame nettles, *Coleus*, and *Asparagus sprengeri*.

Overleaf: Shrubs, climbing plants, roses, geraniums, marigolds, herbs – and even tomatoes – grow in profusion around a simple, wooden deck.

145

Foliage/shade: 1. Brick planting bed, built *in situ.* Water drains through holes to a central gully. The perimeter wall must be separate from any upstanding or building walls. **2.** Thin, stained, plywood panels can be secured to the rails or erected independently to form a screen. **3.** Clear, acrylic panels reduce wind. **4.** The false acacia, *Robinia pseudoacacia* 'Frisia', has early, golden foliage which turns to lime-green during summer. **5.** An eye-catching grouping of *Mahonia japonica*, which has a strong foliage pattern and pale lemon, scented flowers in early spring. **6.** Hellebore, *Helleborus corsicus*, bears green flowers in late spring. **7.** *Elaeagnus pungens* 'Aurea' is an evergreen shrub with bright gold and green foliage. **8.** Plantain lilies, *Hosta.* **9.** The dogwood, *Cornus alba* 'Elegantissima', has variegated foliage and should be cut back in spring to encourage a compact form. **10.** *Cotoneaster horizontalis* is a semi-evergreen with branches arranged in a distinctive, herringbone fashion. **11.** *Osmanthus heterophyllus* has dark green, holly-like leaves. **12.** *Cotoneaster salicifolius floccosus* is an evergreen shrub, with small, slender leaves held on graceful stems. **13.** The leaves of *Parthenocissus henryana*, a type of Virginia creeper, have silvery-white veins. **14.** The holly, *Ilex aquifolium* 'Silver Queen', has silver, variegated leaves. **15.** *Pachysandra terminalis* provides a good, green ground cover.

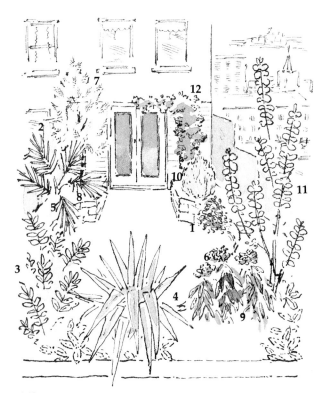

Foliage/sun: 1. Brick planting bed. **2.** Plywood panels. **3.** Golden privet, *Ligustrum ovalifolium* 'Aureomarginatum', is an underrated shrub with bright golden foliage that can be cut back to leave a natural but controlled shape. **4.** *Yucca filamentosa* has striking foliage that forms a strong pattern. **5.** A hardy palm, *Chamaerops humilis*, creates a tropical effect. **6.** Variegated periwinkles, *Vinca major* 'Variegata', tumble over the raised walls. **7.** The mimosas, *Acacia dealbata*, have silver-green, fern-like leaves. **8.** A planting of charming lamb's ears, *Stachys lanata*, is used as ground cover. **9.** The spurge, *Euphorbia griffithii*, has orange heads on bright green foliage. **10.** *Thuja occidentalis* 'Rheingold' is a rounded, golden conifer. **11.** The gum tree, *Eucalyptus gunnii*, has silver-grey foliage. **12.** The climbing rose 'Mrs Sam McCredy' is apricot-orange.

SPECIAL

For fanatics: 1. Greenhouse against the wall; adequate ventilation, preferably automatic, must be provided if it faces south, east or west. It is an excellent retreat during spring and autumn. **2.** A pergola follows the line of the greenhouse and provides shade for: **3.** A garden seat. Cover the pergola with a vine, *Vitis*, or wisteria, *Wistaria*. **4.** Tomatoes in 'Growbags' on patent supports. **5.** A miscellany of tubs and boxes, planted with a generous mixture of alpines, shrubs, herbaceous plants, and annuals—raised in the greenhouse. This is, in fact, a town-dweller's cottage garden. Paint the tubs one colour to co-ordinate the shapes, and establish an asymmetrical balance by using some to separate off: **6.** Space for dining furniture. **7.** Hanging baskets and wall pots complete the charming disarray.

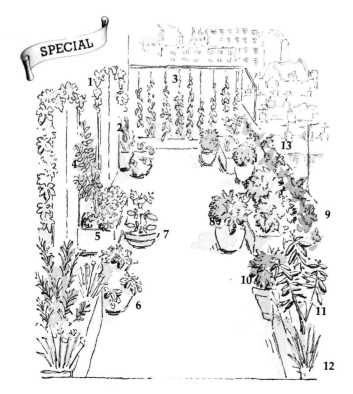

SPECIAL

Useful: 1. Vines, *Vitis vinifera* 'Brandt'; their fresh green foliage breaks the hard lines of the windows. They will produce small but sweet black grapes in summer. **2.** Rosemary, *Rosmarinus officinalis*, is useful for cooking and the bushes are attractive, permanent plants. **3.** Green beans climb supports; a line of lettuces is at their base. **4.** A fan-trained peach, *Prunus persica*. **5.** Parsley, *Petroselinum crispum*. **6.** Strawberry pots planted with the alpine variety 'Baron Solemacher'. **7.** Low half-pots for special herbs like sweet basil, *Ocimum basilicum*. **8.** Outdoor tomatoes in terracotta pots and in the boxes behind them. **9.** A thornless blackberry, *Rubus fruticosus* 'Oregon Thornless', grows from the end and centre boxes. **10.** Bays, *Laurus nobilis*; trim them to shape as you use sprigs. **11.** Lemon-scented verbena, *Lippia citriodora*, has fragrant foliage with which to garnish summer drinks. **12.** Chives, *Allium schoenoprasum*, make a decorative corner in each box. **13.** A clear acrylic or glass screen provides protection from the wind.

SUMMER

Roof gardens look their best from the early summer on, when seasonal plants have been installed and the contrasting green foliage is at its freshest. Plants that provide flowers during these months include *Potentilla*, *Senecio*, *Abelia* and *Buddleia*. For effective foliage, plant grey-leafed *Helichrysum*, and *Ballota* with pale green leaves.

Remember that you will be moving new seasonal plants from the sheltered and often moist environment of a nursery to the harsh reality of exposed and sometimes dry containers or beds. Prepare the soil for the plants by adding a little peat or other organic material, and a slow-release fertilizer. Above all, soak the areas with water. You will find that plants grow rapidly.

Climbing plants are difficult to establish properly. Take every opportunity you have to tie-in all new shoots, spreading them sideways to achieve over-all coverage. There is nothing more unattractive than a gaunt stem terminating in a cluster of tangled leaves.

Check constantly for greenfly (aphids), which can easily over-winter on established plants and spread to seedlings planted among them.

Furniture is important during summer, when a roof garden is often used as an additional room. Purpose-made *in situ* seating is one solution and can double as a design element, breaking up a continuous run of containers and providing a visually attractive feature. Keep a supply of cushions indoors.

A wide range of dining suites and benches is available, ranging from contemporary styles to antique reproductions. Like purpose-made seating, some of this furniture can be regarded as part of the overall design and kept on the roof throughout the year.

Sun-beds range from simple, aluminium models to sophisticated furniture that can be adjusted to an upright position. These are not always totally weatherproof, and are best kept indoors during winter.

Shade: 1. The clematis flowers in early summer, leaving a legacy of silky seed heads for the rest of the season. Prune only if necessary, after flowering. The fuchsia is in flower. **2.** The *Pyracantha* has white flowers in early summer. **3.** Cut and shape the fresh foliage of the spotted laurel at will. **4.** Match or contrast colours in a seasonal planting of half-hardy fuchsias and busy Lizzie, *Impatiens*; include some white-flowering busy Lizzies to create a magical effect at night. **5.** The fresh green foliage of the Japanese maples makes a perfect foil for the seasonal plants. The crimson berries on the *Skimmia* start to ripen in late summer. **6.** Ivy. **7.** Nylon mesh. **8.** A plantain lily, *Hosta glauca*, is planted at the base of the camellia. **9.** Seating.

Sun: 1. Seasonal plantings in boxes suspended from the perimeter rail to leave extra floor space. Co-ordinate the colours with the table umbrella and cushion covers. A yellow and white scheme could include French marigolds, *Tagetes patula*; alyssum; and *Calceolaria*. For pink and red try ivy-leaved geraniums, *Pelargonium peltatum*, and zonal pelargoniums, with petunias. Purple and blue suggestions include geraniums, *Pelargonium* 'William Tell' (zonal), petunias and dark blue lobelia. **2.** The *Abelia* has arching branches of pink and white flowers throughout summer. **3.** Prune and trim the clematis, *C. Montana*, immediately after it has flowered. **4.** 'Ville de Lyon' has carmine red flowers in late summer, mixed with the evergreen foliage of *C. armandii*. **5.** The silver birch has finely cut foliage. It is a strong visual element but allows the sun to shine through. **6.** The Mexican mock orange and lavender are in flower. **7.** The leaf edges of the *Yucca* have curly white threads; flower spikes are probable on this species. **8.** Trellis work. **9.** Nylon netting. **10.** Duckboard.

Scented/summer: 1. Jasmine, *Jasminum officinale*, trained round lattice or steel pyramids. **2.** Plant honeysuckles, *Lonicera halleana* and *L.* 'Serotina', in the rear of containers and wall troughs. **3.** Fill the containers with scented, white tobacco plants, *Nicotiana affinis*. **4.** Vases planted with cherry pie, *Heliotropium*; and lemon-scented geraniums, *Pelargonium tomentosum*. **5.** Vases sown with night-scented stocks, *Matthiola bicornis*. **6.** Plants in hanging baskets provide no perfume but plenty of colour; they can include trailing, half-hardy fuchsias; trailing begonias; or cream and white trailing *Nepeta*. **7.** A 'tent' supported by light steel rods painted pale grey-green provides partial shade for the dining area.

Bedding plants/shade: 1. Clipped edgings of dark green box, *Buxus* 'Suffruticosa'. **2.** Vases planted with half-hardy fuchsias in pinks and purples, and busy Lizzie, *Impatiens sultanii*, in acid pinks. Pink and white trails of *Ampelopsis brevipedunculata* 'Elegans' heighten the arrangements. **3.** *Cobaea scandens*, will scramble up the walls with some support, but will flower only in a good light. **4.** The borders are planted with palest pink busy Lizzies, *Impatiens sultanii*, backed by a mass of pale pink, cerise, and white tobacco plants, *Nicotiana affinis* 'Sensation Mixed'; and bells of Ireland, *Molucella laevis*; their lime green leaves contrast especially well with pink flowers. **5.** Fence panels are painted very pale blue-green to produce the illusion of a natural background but in an even shadier situation the tone could be yet lighter.

Bedding plants/sun: 1. The clipped edging around the containers is *Santolina chamaecyparissus*, with silver foliage and lemon yellow flowers. **2.** Containers are filled with geraniums, *Pelargonium* 'Orange Fizz' (zonal); nasturtiums, *Tropaeolum majus*; pale blue, trailing lobelia; petunias *P.* 'Brass Band'; and grey, trailing *Helichrysum petiolatum*. **3.** The annual climbers are black-eyed Susan, *Thunbergia alata*, with black-centred, brilliant orange flowers. **4.** Border areas are edged with pale blue lobelia and filled with a miscellany of French marigolds, *Tagetes patula*, in lemon and orange; white tobacco plants, *Nicotiana affinis*; and marguerites, *Felicia amelloides*. **5.** The side fencing panels are plywood, cut with a jigsaw to simulate a hedge top and stained very dark green. Alternatively, if your roof could support the soil to sustain it, you could have a real hedge of yew, *Taxus baccata*.

Low maintenance/shade: 1. *Griselinia littoralis* has an upright growing form and bright green leaves. **2.** The common ivy, *Hedera helix*, can grow up and over the screen, depending on the height of the building and wind velocity. **3.** The self-clinging Virginia creeper, *Parthenocissus quinquefolia*, is green in summer. **4.** A mixed border of *Ilex crenata*; plantain lilies, *Hosta fortunei*; and *Viburnum tinus*. **5.** The bamboos, *Arundinaria nitida*, create an elegant, vertical line against the wall. **6.** Containers under the built-in seat allow the Virginia creeper to grow up the wall. **7.** The secret of this garden's success is a tap linked to an automatic watering system or simple sprinkler hose. **8.** The seat and table are placed to catch the morning sun.

Low maintenance/sun: This plan uses plants with white and yellow flowers. **1.** Containers planted with *Potentilla* 'Primrose Beauty', which has grey-green foliage. **2.** *Senecio greyi* produces yellow flowers and silver-grey foliage. **3.** *Olearia* x *haastii* has white, daisy-like flowers and grey-green foliage. **4.** *Buddleia davidii*. Cut it back in early spring to keep it reasonably compact—but eye-catching. **5.** The handsome, leathery foliage of *Viburnum davidii* looks best after new spring growth. It produces insignificant white flowers. **6.** Although the rail is covered with trellis and a nylon-mesh windbreak, climbing plants have a hard task covering the entire perimeter. To maintain the colour scheme, plant a white clematis, *Clematis montana* 'Alba', and a white, evergreen honeysuckle, *Lonicera halleana*. **7.** One of the recently introduced small varieties of *Phormium*, with cream leaves; it creates a stiff, architectural contrast to the soft shapes of other foliage. **8.** Southernwood, *Artemisia abrotanum*, can be clipped back in spring and will produce an abundance of silver-grey foliage in summer. **9.** A screen, up to 6½ ft (about two metres) high, gives shelter from the wind and encloses: **10.** The fitted seating area. **11.** Automatic watering system or simple sprinkler hose attached to tap. All the pots are in straight lines, so the essential—and endless—watering can be easily carried out.

AUTUMN WINTER

Although the soft green look of summer begins to harden as the autumn approaches, plants like fuchsias, busy Lizzie, begonias and geraniums continue to flower until the first frost takes its toll. Late-flowering shrubs that are particularly suitable for roof gardens include *Fatsia* with its strong foliage form surmounted by cream candelabra-like blooms. Firethorns and varieties of *Cotoneaster* contribute a profusion of berries.

Fill spaces between shrubs with chrysanthemums or ornamental peppers, bought in flower or fruit from a nursery or garden centre. Alternatively, plan ahead and buy pots of chrysanthemum plants in late spring, using them in inconspicuous corners to provide additional greenery during summer before moving them to their autumn positions.

Prune climbing roses in autumn, tying new, strong shoots firmly into trellis work or other supports. Trim back weaker shoots and any that have flowered to within three or four buds of a main stem.

Remove summer seasonal plantings in mid-autumn to make room for spring plants. First cultivate the soil as deeply as possible with a hand fork, incorporating bone-meal. It will then be easier to plant bulbs at an even depth, ensuring consistent flowers.

To ensure colour throughout winter, fill containers with bulbs and overplant them with winter cherries. Make sure the soil doesn't dry out, or the berries will shrivel and the leaves droop. If the containers are kept moist and the winter stays mild, the winter cherries will survive until spring, when the bulbs emerge.

Keep an eye on your roof garden during winter, even if some areas are not immediately visible from the house. Repair trellis panels if necessary, tie in plants worked loose by winter gales – and always make sure planting areas are adequately moist.

Shade: 1. Clematis. The fuchsia at its base dies down during winter; prune to tidy early in the season, but only cut back hard in spring when you can determine how far down the wood has died back. **2.** The red berries of the *Pyracantha* last through autumn into early winter. The leaves will hold a little longer. **3.** The leaves of the spotted laurel provide colour in winter. **4.** Fuchsias last into autumn. Busy Lizzie dies when the first frosts come. Remove the plants and fill the space with narcissus bulbs. Plant winter cherries, *Solanum capsicastrum*, on top. A few short ivies, *Hedera*, at the containers' sides will break the bleak lines during winter and can be incorporated into the next season's planting. **5.** The leaves of the Japanese maples turn golden yellow, complementing the berries on the *Skimmia*. **6.** Ivy. **7.** Nylon mesh. **8.** Camellia. **9.** Seating.

Sun: 1. Some geraniums survive but should be moved by mid-autumn to make room for narcissus and tulip bulbs; forget-me-nots, *Myosotis*; and wallflowers, *Cheiranthus*. **2.** In a mild autumn the *Abelia* continues to flower until the middle of the season. **3.** Tidy errant shoots on the clematis, *C. Montana*, but allow one or two to trail across part of the window to create a winter silhouette. **4.** *C.* 'Ville de Lyon' carries its seed heads; *C. armandii* begins to flower very early in spring. **5.** The foliage of the silver birch turns yellow. **6.** Trim the lavender after flowering; remove all seed heads and shape the plant as necessary. **7.** There are seed heads on the *Yucca.* **8.** Make sure the trellis is stable well before the winter winds set in. **9.** Nylon netting. **10.** Clean out leaves from under the duckboard. Always check that the drain is kept free.

SPECIAL

Contrasting colours: 1, 2. Containers and seat are painted gloss white. **3.** Dark green, pyramid-shaped bay trees. **4.** Mop-headed bays. **5.** Dark green Persian ivy, *Hedera colchica*, on white stucco wall. **6.** Scarlet geraniums (zonal pelargoniums) in summer; red tulips 'Fusilier' in spring. Boxes are edged with green ivy, *Hedera*.

OVERWINTERING GERANIUMS

Roof gardens often have micro-climates that allow geraniums planted in vases and other containers to survive all but the harshest winters. Half-hardy perennials, they can in fact improve substantially if they are grown on into a second year.

Trim them lightly in mid-autumn and reduce water until the soil in the container is almost dry. This is important – wet soil will heighten their susceptibility to frost damage. Trim them to an even shape in mid-spring, and then increase their water again. Encourage growth by applying a liquid fertilizer from late spring onwards.

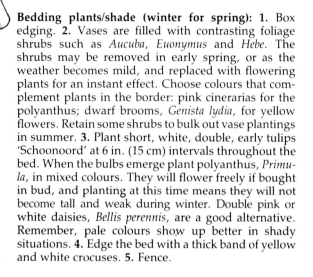

Bedding plants/shade (winter for spring): 1. Box edging. **2.** Vases are filled with contrasting foliage shrubs such as *Aucuba*, *Euonymus* and *Hebe*. The shrubs may be removed in early spring, or as the weather becomes mild, and replaced with flowering plants for an instant effect. Choose colours that complement plants in the border: pink cinerarias for the polyanthus; dwarf brooms, *Genista lydia*, for yellow flowers. Retain some shrubs to bulk out vase plantings in summer. **3.** Plant short, white, double, early tulips 'Schoonoord' at 6 in. (15 cm) intervals throughout the bed. When the bulbs emerge plant polyanthus, *Primula*, in mixed colours. They will flower freely if bought in bud, and planting at this time means they will not become tall and weak during winter. Double pink or white daisies, *Bellis perennis*, are a good alternative. Remember, pale colours show up better in shady situations. **4.** Edge the bed with a thick band of yellow and white crocuses. **5.** Fence.

Bedding plants/sun (winter to spring): 1. *Santolina* remains throughout winter. **2.** Containers are filled with clear yellow, early narcissi 'February Gold' and overplanted with winter cherries, *Solanum capsicastrum*; the display will be finished by early spring. **3.** The main border edging is forget-me-nots, *Myosotis*. **4.** Wallflowers, *Cheiranthus*, mixed with tulips, 'Triumph' type. **5.** Fencing panels or hedge.

For the disabled: 1. Raised beds for easy access. **2.** Mesh screens and **3.** Acrylic screens give protection against the wind. The mesh screens allow some sunlight through. **4.** The 'lost' area at the side is panelled out to avoid the need to clear leaves. **5.** Trailing plants hang over, and soften, the tall sides of the planters. Try: aubretia; *Cotoneaster dammeri*; alyssum, *A. saxatile*; bellflowers, *Campanula*; and various ivies, *Hedera helix*. Plant narcissi, tulips and hyacinths for spring. Summer plantings could include salvia and marigolds, *Tagetes*. Chrysanthemums, 'Korean' type, planted in early summer will flower in autumn. **6.** Climbers tumble over rail. **7.** Sculpture.

Roof light: This can often be partially covered without adversely affecting light in the room below. **1.** Roof light. **2.** Deep container. **3.** Trellis or other open-mesh support. **4.** Bracket to support horizontal bearer. **5.** Low boxes containing evergreen plants.

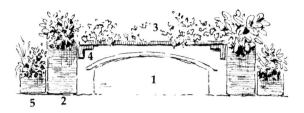

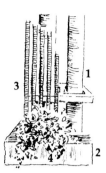

Vertical pipes: 1. Pipes. **2.** A simple clamping device holds a metal strip or wood to take vertical battens, and is repeated higher up the pipe. **3.** Vertical battens. **4.** Box for climbing plants and supporting foliage.

This scheme can also be used to disguise chimney stacks.

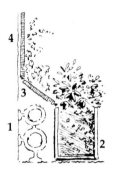

Horizontal pipes: 1. Pipes. **2.** Deep box containing compost and plants; include scrambling types to scramble on: **3.** Sloping trellis that bridges the gap between the box and: **4.** Trellis panel on the wall.

RAISED PLANTER

This *in situ* box is also suitable for disabled gardeners. **1.** Side members 6in. high by 1in. deep (15cm by 2.5cm), screwed to: **2.** Corner post. **3.** Brass screws in cups are located in all side members. **4.** Spacer batten leaves horizontal reveal. **5.** Raising batten across the base. **6.** Plastic foam slabs. **7.** Capping secures: **8.** Plastic lining with holes in base for drainage. **9.** Compost. **10.** Lightweight drainage layer. **11.** Fibreglass blanket separates compost and drainage.

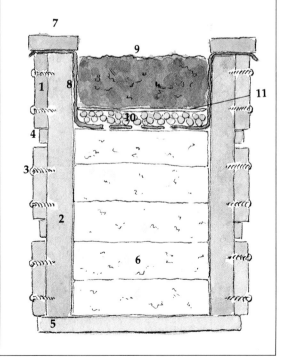

INDEX

Plants are indexed under both common names, where relevant, and botanical names. In addition, common names are given in brackets after the botanical names and page numbers for both are included in these entries; *italic* numbers refer to the pages on which names appear in Latin. **Bold** numbers refer to photographs.

159

Acknowledgements

The publishers would like to thank the following for their contribution to this book

Jessica Strang; pages
34/35, 42; right, 48, 62/63, 83, 88, 98, 114/115, 134, 138/139, 140.
Susan Griggs Agency; Title page
Michael Boys, contents page
Monique Jacot, 42 Adam Woolfit.
Lorraine Johnson pages 82, 118.
Christopher Drew Back Cover, 146/147
Don Nicholson pages 24, 64, 104.